The Collected Works of Edith Stein

VIII

The Collected Works
of
EDITH STEIN

Sister Teresa Benedicta of the Cross
Discalced Carmelite
1891–1942

Edited by
Dr. L. Gelber
and
Michael Linssen, O.C.D.

Volume Eight

ICS Publications
Institute of Carmelite Studies
Washington, D.C.
2000

EDITH STEIN

Sister Teresa Benedicta of the Cross
Discalced Carmelite

KNOWLEDGE AND FAITH

Translated by Walter Redmond

ICS Publications
Institute of Carmelite Studies
Washington, D.C.
2000

The original of this work was published in German by the
Archivum Carmelitanum Edith Stein under the title
Erkenntnis und Glaube
Band XV of *Edith Steins Werke*
Translation authorized.
© Verlag Herder, Freiburg im Breisgau 1993

With the permission of the Archivum Carmelitanum Edith Stein
and Max Niemeyer Verlag, an English translation of Edith Stein's
article "Husserls Phänomenologie und die Philosophie des hl.
Thomas v. Aquino. Versuch einer Gegenüberstellung" has been
added to the ICS Publications edition. This article originally appeared in *Festschrift Edmund Husserl zum 70. Geburtstag gewidmet,
1929,* supplement of *Jahrbuch für Philosophie und phänomenologische
Forschung.* Second edition © Max Niemeyer Verlag Tübingen 1974.

*Cover designed by Mother Mary Joseph, O.C.D.,
of the Carmel of Port Tobacco*

Library of Congress Cataloging-in-Publication Data

Stein, Edith, 1891–1942
  [Erkenntnis und Glaube. English]
  Knowledge and faith / edited by L. Gelber and Michael
  Linssen; translated by Walter Redmond.
    p. cm. — (The collected works of Edith Stein; v. 8)
  Includes bibliographical references (p.) and index.
  Contents: Husserl and Aquinas—Knowledge, truth,
  being—Actual and ideal being, species, type and likeness
  (fragment)—Sketch of a foreword to Finite and eternal
  being (fragment)—Ways to know God.
    ISBN 0–935216–71–5 (alk. paper: paperback)
    1. Philosophy and religion. 2. God—knowableness.
  I. Gelber, Lucy. II. Linssen, Michael. III. Title.

B3332.S672 E54 1986 vol. 8
[BR 100]
193 s—dc21
[231'.042]   99–046693

Table of Contents

Translator's Note

THIS ENGLISH EDITION of volume 15 of *Edith Steins Werke* includes one work not contained in *Erkenntnis und Glaube*: the monograph "An Attempt to Contrast Husserl's Phenomenology and the Philosophy of St. Thomas Aquinas." On the occasion of Husserl's seventieth birthday St. Teresa Benedicta of the Cross composed an imaginary dialogue between her two "masters," Edmund Husserl and St. Thomas Aquinas, and entitled it "What is Philosophy? A Conversation between Edmund Husserl and Thomas Aquinas." At the suggestion of philosopher Martin Heidegger, she reworked this dialogue into an article for a *Festschrift*, or commemorative issue in Husserl's honor, of the journal of phenomenology *Jahrbuch für Philosophie und phänomenologische Forschung.* The article appeared in 1929, but the original dialogue was published for the first time only in 1993 in *Erkenntnis und Glaube.* Both versions are printed here in parallel columns under the heading "Husserl and Aquinas: A Comparison," with the original dialogue labeled "Version A," and the later article labeled "Version B."

"Ways to Know God," first published in English in the journal *The Thomist*, in a translation by Edith Stein's friend Rudolf Allers, appears here in an entirely new translation.

Curly brackets enclose additions by the German editor as well as the page numbers of the German edition of *Erkenntnis und Glaube* (or the journal and article page numbers separated by a slash in the case of the *Festschrift* article, i.e., version B of "What is Philosophy?"). Translator's additions appear in square brackets; in particular, throughout Stein's texts subheadings by the translator have been added in square brackets to help guide the reader.

The translator has endeavored to avoid specialist terms as much as possible, but readers familiar with phenomenology and Thomism should have no difficulty in following the technical meaning. In the case of sensitive translations the basic German word is appended, italicized and in square brackets (often only the first time the word occurs); in some cases boldface is also used to indicate that part of the German word which Edith Stein herself italicized for emphasis. In quotations of St. Thomas and Pseudo-Dionysius, Edith Stein's translations have been followed. *Seiendes* is rendered as (a particular) "be-ing" (hyphenated) to distinguish it from *Sein*, "being" (in general); *Wesen* appears as "being" when it has this particular sense, but it may also mean "essence."

WALTER REDMOND
Austin, Texas

Foreword to the German Edition

THE PRESENT VOLUME, the fifteenth of the German works of Edith Stein, is one more substantial contribution to the study of thought and faith. The writings it brings together span the years 1929–1941, after she finished her translation of St. Thomas Aquinas's *De Veritate* and immediately before and after she wrote *Finite and Eternal Being.* They cover her intellectual and spiritual journey from her first turning to Augustine and Dionysius the Areopagite, into the final phase of a well-defined religious philosophy, to faith and knowledge. This will be especially clear in "Ways to Know God," which immediately preceded *Science of the Cross,* her last, unfinished, work; it appears here in a revised and enlarged re-edition.

Edith Stein's philosophical activity has no breaks although it does show significant development. As a young student and freethinker in religion she turned to the phenomenology of Edmund Husserl. However, her strict religious upbringing as a child in a Jewish home and her later encounter with Catholic thinking through her reading and conversations sparked a desire for a view of life based on religion—which now was Christianity. Without foregoing the method of phenomenological analysis and ever grounded on Thomistic principles and reasoning, she came to value, in accord with the Carmelite approach to faith, first the natural and then the mystical experience of God.

Our sincerest thanks to Dr. Walter Biemel for his help in reconstructing "Ways to Know God" from unpublished material.

MICHAEL LINSSEN, O.C.D.
Geleen Carmel
November 1, 1992

Foreword to the ICS Edition

IN HIS RECENT ENCYCLICAL on the relationship between faith and reason, *Fides et Ratio,* Pope John Paul II lists Edith Stein (St. Teresa Benedicta of the Cross, O.C.D.) among those modern thinkers who offer "significant examples of a process of philosophical enquiry which was enriched by engaging the data of faith."[1] And he adds, "One thing is certain: attention to the spiritual journey of these masters can only give greater momentum to both the search for truth and the effort to apply the results of that search to the service of humanity."[2] In that vein, the present volume provides an anthology of shorter writings by Edith Stein that reveal much about her efforts, after her conversion from atheism, to integrate her new-found Christian faith with her previous training in the modern philosophical movement known as phenomenology, to which she was an important early contributor.

Knowledge and Faith, the eighth entry in the ICS Publications series of "The Collected Works of Edith Stein," is a translation of volume 15 of the German edition of *Edith Steins Werke,* with one important addition. As Professor Walter Redmond explains in his "Translator's Note," the first piece in this anthology, here entitled "What Is Philosophy? A Conversation between Edmund Husserl and Thomas Aquinas," was Edith Stein's invited contribution to a special issue of the *Jahrbuch für Philosophie und phänomenologische Forschung,* begun by Edmund Husserl (1859–1938) and published by Max Niemeyer Verlag in Tübingen, Germany. This issue was to be a *Festschrift* marking Husserl's seventieth birthday, with essays by his most prominent students (including also Martin Heidegger, Roman Ingarden, Alexandre Koyré, and Hedwig Conrad-Martius). As the subtitle indicates, Edith Stein originally composed her piece in the form of an imaginary dialogue between Husserl, as founder of the phenomenological movement, and Aquinas, as preeminent spokeman for Thomism and the Catholic philosophical tradition. However, Martin Heidegger, the editor of the *Festschrift*, returned the dialogue to its author, asking for a more "neutral" treatment of the subject matter.[3] Stein rewrote her piece as an essay, which was then accepted and appeared in the 1929 *Festschrift*. The original dialogue version, however, remained unpublished until its inclusion in *Erkenntnis und Glaube*. Through the kindness of the Archivum Carmelitanum Edith Stein and Max Niemeyer Verlag, we are now able to present both versions here together for the first time, in parallel columns so that readers may more easily compare them. Stein's original attempt in dialogue form is here marked as "Version A," while the revised essay as published in the Husserl *Festschrift* is marked "Version B."

"Ways to Know God," the fifth and final selection in this anthology, has an even more unusual history. The statement in the "Editor's Preface" below that "Edith Stein was working on this article for the American journal *The Thomist* in 1940–1941"[4] omits a number of important steps in its circuitous journey toward publication, as materials recently uncovered in the archives of the State University of New York at Buffalo confirm. There, among the papers of philosophy professor Marvin Farber,[5] is an extensive correspondence with Fritz Kaufmann, philosopher and friend of Edith Stein from their days together as members of the "Göttingen Circle" of phenomenologists; driven from his academic position at the University of Freiburg by the anti-Semitic policies of the Nazis, Kaufmann had come to the United States in 1937 and joined the faculty of Northwestern University. By 1939, Kaufmann and Farber were corresponding frequently about the establishment of the International Phenomenological Society and its journal, *Philosophy and Phenomenological Research,* of which Farber was the founding editor and Kaufmann a member of the Board of Editors.

In early 1940, Marvin Farber had written to Edith Stein in Echt, informing her of the newly formed International Phenomenological Society, and inviting her to join and to contribute to its journal. On April 4, Edith Stein wrote back:

> Heartfelt thanks for your friendly letter of February 28 and the invitation to take part in the newly founded society about which Mrs. Husserl has already written to me. Naturally, as a

former student and collaborator of Husserl, I will have great interest in seeing the society thrive. As for membership, it has little
advantage for a woman who is a religious: not only am I unable
to pay the fee, but I would also never be able to participate in an
event since I live in papal enclosure and cannot travel, in fact I
never leave the house. Also since the monastic daily schedule
leaves me next to no time for literary work, cooperating with the
magazine would also hardly be possible. But I will be glad to call
attention to it whenever the opportunity arises to do so.[6]

Stein's letter goes on to ask his help in finding a U.S. publisher
for *Finite and Eternal Being*, and mentions relatives and friends (including Fritz Kaufmann) living in North America.

Marvin Farber next contacted Fritz Kaufmann, informing him
of Stein's reply, and asking his advice.[7] On May 7, 1940, Kaufmann
responded:

There is no doubt at all that *Edith Stein* should become a member of
our society even though she may be unable to pay her contribution.
I say this not only because she has been a most beloved friend of
mine, but her first works belong to the most valuable and authen-
tic contribution to phenomenology in the line of the *Ideen*. Above
all, she has been one of the most devoted friends of Husserl and
served him during the war in the most unselfish way not only as
a secretary but also—during a grave malady of his—as his nurse.
We honor Husserl's memory in asking her to be with us.[8]

Farber heeded this suggestion and on May 9 wrote to "Sister
Theresia Benedicta a Cruce" announcing that:

The Council of the Phenomenological Society has voted to make
you a charter member of the organization, and to send you a
copy of the journal without charge. Your notable record of schol-
arship in this field, and your great interest in its continued
progress, leads us to welcome and value your membership.... I
hope that you will sincerely consider sending us an essay for the
journal that is based upon any work that you have done in the
past, and that you will think of this as *our* undertaking.[9]

Edith Stein wrote back on November 4, 1940, thanking Farber "sincerely for making me a member of your Phenomenological Society."[10] Then, several months later, in a postcard dated April 4, 1940,

she picks up on his earlier invitation to submit an essay for publication in *Philosophy and Phenomenological Research.*

> I have been engaged for some months in collecting material for
> a major work about Dionysius the Areopagite. Now I have begun
> to write something from that quarter which I could send you as a
> contribution: "Ways to Know God according to the Teaching of
> the Areopagite." I believe you have made your parameters wide
> enough to include something like this. My superiors do leave me
> full liberty; but it is, of course, self-evident that I cannot write on
> anything that has nothing at all to do with our life.[11]

After receiving a warm response to this from Marvin Farber,[12]
Stein wrote again on September 12, 1941:

> Your friendly card of May 9 reached me in a relatively short
> time (that is, in about a month). I did not answer earlier because
> I wanted to send you the promised contribution [i.e., "Ways to
> Know God"] for the periodical. And now I am taking a chance
> on sending it. You will forgive me for not sending my best copy.
> I am unable to judge myself whether it is suitable for your peri-
> odical.... I hope the article is not all too long for you. Much that
> is dispensable I have already struck out. I have marked the place
> [of another section] that could be deleted. I would be grateful
> to have word from you soon after you receive [the article]. If I do
> not receive confirmation of its reception by January 1 I will as-
> sume it has not reached you and that I am free to make other use
> of the article. In case you do receive and accept it, would it be all
> right with you if, eventually, it were to appear here in a Dutch
> translation? Would it be possible that Fritz Kaufmann take over
> any corrections? Or would you wish to do that yourself?
>   With best wishes,
>   your grateful Sr. Teresia Benedicta a Cruce, O.C.D.[13]

Marvin Farber quickly wrote back acknowledging receipt of the
article,[14] and then consulted Fritz Kaufmann for his opinion of it.
On November 7, 1941, Kaufmann responded, recommending the
essay for publication, but with some reservations:

> Edith Stein's paper is an interesting and thoroughgoing
> analysis of the stages of religious experience with the help of phe-
> nomenological categories as provided for by the first generation

of phenomenologists. There is no more dogmatism in it than we had to expect as unavoidable under the present circumstances.... The paper is lucid, well written and contains a number of fine remarks. Without being too enthusiasic about it, I recommend its publication.... I made already many corrections of obvious misprints in the manuscript. In addition I marked on the margins...some slight changes or additions that seem necessary to me for one reason or the other. On [page] 3 I would delete not only the two passages which [Edith Stein] suggests herself but also the sentence between—which seems to contradict a statement on [page] 2.[15]

Farber also sought the opinion of another disciple of Husserl, Alfred Schütz, who (in a letter of May 3, 1942) called Edith Stein's essay "a fine paper" but recommended that it be published elsewhere, since "it does not fit in the frame of our journal, being purely theological."[16] Farber answered Schütz on May 9: "Your suggestion concerning Edith Stein's paper is a very good one, I think, and I shall try to interest some other journal in it."[17] Evidently, however, Farber had not found a translator or another journal by June, when Kaufmann wrote expressing his regret at Farber's decision not to publish the article, in German, in *Philosophy and Phenomenological Research.*[18] Less than eight weeks later, unbeknownst to her friends in the United States, Edith Stein was arrested and sent to the gas chambers of the Auschwitz concentration camp, where she died on August 9, 1942.

There the matter apparently remained until 1944, when Farber and Kaufmann were discussing a manuscript submitted by James Collins. In a letter of March 30, Kaufmann observed: "It is a pity that we did not know of this man when we negotiated with Edith Stein about her book and some articles of hers. (By the way what has been the destiny of her paper on Dionysius Areopagita I read years ago?).... Perhaps it is not too late even now?"[19] Farber responded on April 6 that "Collins is connected with Catholic University in Washington.... I shall, as soon as I can get to it, take up the Edith Stein matter with him...."[20]

In the end, the article was sent to another member of the Catholic University faculty, the noted philosopher-psychologist Rudolf Allers, who had known Edith Stein back in Germany. He wrote to Marvin Farber on September 5, 1945:

I thank you for your card and I shall be very glad to look at the [manuscript] of Edith Stein. There are, of course, possibilities for publishing it either in *The Thomist* or in *The New Scholasticism,* if it should prove suitable. Should I feel so, I shall take care of having the article translated, or I may translate it myself.... I have no reliable news on Edith Stein. There have been rumors, and they are countenanced by the Carmelite Fathers—though I do not know on what evidence—that she had been taken by the Germans away from the convent in Holland and put in a concentration camp in Poland where she is said to have died. There is, however, no official confirmation.[21]

Allers wrote again to Farber on October 9, acknowledging receipt of the manuscript:

I have not yet, as you will understand, read the article, but I have rapidly looked through it. It seems to me, at first sight, that it might be quite suitable for publication, for instance in *The Thomist.* But it may need some cutting out of certain passages which seem to be rather long and even a little prolix. In any case, if the article is going to be printed, I would like to mention the fact that you received it first and handed it over to me.... Translating Dr. Stein's article will not prove an easy task. Certain idiomatic peculiarities lend themselves but badly to an exact rendering in English. So, for instance, the use she makes of the linguistic kinship of "Bild," "Gebilde," "bilden," for which there is no equivalent. However, I shall do my best.[22]

After countless delays, then, "Ways to Know God" appeared at last in the July 1946 issue of *The Thomist,* in an English translation by Rudolf Allers. Included with the article was the preliminary note Allers had requested, clearly indicating that Stein's manuscript had been submitted originally not to *The Thomist* but "to Professor Marvin Farber, the editor of the *Journal of Philosophy and Phenomenological Research,* in the fall of 1941."[23] In the meantime, the editor of the present volume, Dr. Lucy Gelber, had arranged for the publication of "Wege der Gotteserkenntnis" in the February 1946 issue of *Tijdschrift voor Philosophie.*[24] Thus, by a matter of a few months, the work Edith Stein had originally intended for an American journal ended up being published first in Louvain (Belgium), in her original German.

Commendably, with the cooperation of *The Thomist,* the Edith Stein Guild of New York City has continued to make the Allers translation of "Ways to Know God" available in reprint pamphlet form.[25] Unfortunately, diligent searches in various archives and among the papers of Rudolf Allers have so far failed to turn up the manuscript from which he was working, and so we may never know precisely which changes and corrections he or Fritz Kaufmann introduced. But we are pleased to present for the first time a fresh English translation of the full text, from the original German, amplified with important passages excised from previously published versions. There readers will find, for example, Edith Stein's intriguing comments on various forms of atheism, reflections that hint at her own inner journey to faith.

Finally, in addition to the translator and German editors, various people deserve special thanks for their contribution to this volume, including the editors of *The Thomist;* Christopher Densmore, archivist of the University at Buffalo, who helped locate the relevant materials among the voluminous papers of Marvin Farber; Sr. Josephine Koeppel, O.C.D., who first suggested a visit to these archives, and provided the English translation of the previously unpublished Stein letters found therein; Mrs. Christel Allers, who allowed us to examine the surviving papers of her father-in-law, Rudolf Allers; Stephen Tiano, who typeset the book; and John Sullivan, O.C.D., whose advice and knowledge of Edith Stein proved invaluable. To quote again the words of Pope John Paul II, may this latest entry among "The Collected Works of Edith Stein" enable readers to devote greater "attention to the spiritual journey" of St. Teresa Benedicta of the Cross, Edith Stein, so that they may learn from her how to "search for truth" ever more faithfully, and "apply the results of that search to the service of humanity."[26]

STEVEN PAYNE, OCD
Editor-in-Chief
ICS Publications

Editor's Introduction

THIS VOLUME, the fifteenth of *Edith Steins Werke*, contains five different philosophical writings composed between 1929 and 1941. They have not previously been published except for "Wege der Gotteserkenntnis" [Ways to Know God], written in 1940–1941 in the Carmelite convent of Echt in the Netherlands for the American journal *The Thomist* and published here in revised and enlarged form.[1]

The longest selection is the original version of "Husserls Phänomenologie und die Philosophie des hl. Thomas von Aquino: Versuch einer Gegenüberstellung" [An Attempt to Contrast Husserl's Phenomenology and the Philosophy of St. Thomas Aquinas], a contribution to the journal of her teacher Edmund Husserl. Edith Stein wrote the first version of this article in dialogue form and entitled it "Was ist Philosophie?—Ein Gespräch zwischen Edmund Husserl und Thomas von Aquino" [What is Philosophy?—A Conversation between Edmund Husserl and Thomas Aquinas]. It has been completely reconstructed from unpublished material and is made available here for the first time.

Also published for the first time are "Erkenntnis—Wahrheit—Sein" [Knowledge, Truth, Being], notes for her lecture course in Münster in 1932–1933, "Aktuelles und ideales Sein—Species—Urbild und Abbild" [Actual and Ideal Being, Species, Type and Likeness], a fragment on the topic of her *Potenz und Akt* [Potency and Act] (Freiburg i. Br., 1931–1932) as well as her Münster lectures, and a fragment of a draft of the foreword to her principal work *Endliches und Ewiges Sein* [Finite and Eternal Being] (1936).

All texts have been authenticated by comparison with Edith Stein's handwriting. The manuscripts are found in the Archivum Carmelitanum Edith Stein in Brussels.[2]

1. What is Philosophy?

"An Attempt to Contrast Husserl's Phenomenology and the Philosophy of St. Thomas Aquinas" in the *Festschrift Edmund Husserl* [a special issue of the *Jahrbuch für Philosophie und phänomenologische Forschung* to commemorate Husserl's seventieth birthday] is one of the most widely read works of Edith Stein. It was known that the article was an extensive revision of a previous dialogue entitled "What is Philosophy? A Conversation between Edmund Husserl and Thomas Aquinas," but the content and style of the original remained unfamiliar, and it appears in print here for the first time.

The text of the dialogue was reconstructed in the following way: Edith Stein made the changes required for publication on the manuscript of the first version, and they had to be isolated in order to restore the original text. The task turned out to be much more difficult than a glance at the manuscript would suggest, since both the original and the changes are written with the same ink and in the same handwriting. So every tiny detail had to be scrutinized to tell whether cuts and inserts belonged to the original or to the revision. We trust nonetheless that our procedure has accurately restored the original wording.

The Archivum Carmelitanum Edith Stein contains the following:

a) The complete manuscript of the first and second (original plus changes) versions of the article, under the call number AI 9; 42 sheets, 21 x 16.5 cm., numbered 1–75 plus two additional sheets, one numbered 1–2. Latin script, ink, most sheets double-sided.

b) The printed version in the *Festschrift Edmund Husserl zum 70. Geburtstag gewidmet,* supplement of the *Jahrbuch für Philosophie und phänomenologische Forschung* (Halle a.d. Saale: Max Niemeyer Verlag, 1929): 315–338. Also under the call number AI 9.

c) An obviously discarded sheet containing a fragment from the first version, one of the items salvaged from the ruins of the Dutch monastery at Herkenbosch, under the call number AI 4, "loose sheets." A single sheet, 21 x 16.5 cm., page number 68. Latin script, ink, two-sided.

2. Knowledge, Truth, Being

The Archivum Carmelitanum Edith Stein contains a manuscript in Edith Stein's handwriting under the heading "Knowledge, Truth, Being," possibly part of a larger study.

Dr. Hans Brunnengräber, M.D., Ph.D., made the text available to us 30 years ago and asked us to consider it when her works would be published, and we are now happy to oblige. He was a colleague of Edith Stein at the Marianum in Münster from 1931 to 1933 (see letters 135 and 161, *Self-Portrait in Letters, 1916–1942* [volume 5 of the ICS edition of Stein's Collected Works]) and received the manuscript from her personally. To judge from its content and the paper it is written on, it is closely related to sections viii and ix of the course she taught in Münster in 1932–1933 (the manuscript of the course is in the Archivum Carmelitanum Edith Stein, shelf-mark AI 2, and [was] published as volume 16 of *Edith Steins Werke* [*Der Aufbau der menschlichen Person*, edited by Lucy Gelber and Michael Linssen (Freiburg: Herder, 1994)]). The style suggests, however, that the text published here was not intended for lectures.

Description: Call number AI 12 II, 17 sheets, 21.5 x 17 cm. Latin script, ink, written on the back of the typewritten sheets of her *De Veritate* translation (she also used these sheets for her Münster lectures of 1932–1933, manuscript AI 2; the page numbers are complementary).

The individual parts are ordered as Edith Stein indicated. She later supplemented her treatise on truth with pages 14, 15, and 16 on different quality paper; from page 17 she continued using the sheets of the *De Veritate* translation.

3. Actual and Ideal Being, Species, Type and Likeness

There is no information on the origin and date of this fragment from Edith Stein's unpublished writings. Since we know that she was in the habit of discarding her manuscripts after they were published, from the archivists' viewpoint we can assume either that these pages formed part of a lost manuscript or else that they were salvaged from a work not intended for publication and kept for further use because of their importance to her.

The first possibility cannot be pursued here because Edith Stein never compiled a list of her works. The second merits closer attention. The subject of the manuscript is closely allied to *Potency and Act* (in the Archivum Carmelitanum Edith Stein, shelf-number AI 4), the study with which she tried unsuccessfully to qualify as a lecturer in the University of Freiburg i. Br. in 1931–1932. The texts themselves, however, do not belong to this study. They are also related in content to the manuscript AI 12 II "Knowledge, Truth, Being" mentioned above, but the paper differs in quality and color. AI 12 II was written in Münster and AI 4 at a later date when Edith Stein was working on her translation of the writings of the Areopagite. The fragment should be grouped with the Münster course on the basis of its content as well; but it is not a discarded part of this manuscript.

Description: Call number AI 4, "Loose Sheets." 12 sheets, 21 x 16.5 cm. Pagination: 56 and 56a, 57a–c, 58a–e, 76a–b. Latin script, ink, one-sided.

4. *Fragment of a draft of the foreword to* Finite and Eternal Being

This first draft bears the date May 20, 1935 and the final, printed, foreword is dated September 1, 1936 (see, *Endliches und ewiges Sein*, volume 2 of her German works). "Cologne-Lindenthal" is the place given in both versions. Presumably Edith Stein kept the sheet because its content was important to her. It was salvaged from the ruins of the Herkenbosch convent and is a valuable biographical record supplementing the final copy of the foreword.

One double sheet, 21.5 x 16.5 cm. Pagination: 4a and 4b. Latin. script, ink, one-sided.

5. *Ways to Know God*

According to her prioress, Edith Stein was working on this article for the American journal *The Thomist* in 1940–1941 in the Dutch Carmelite convent at Echt.[3] She completed it immediately before her *Science of the Cross* (*Kreuzeswissenschaft*, volume 1 of her German works), her last, unfinished, work, which the article anticipates. The editors of this journal of the Dominican Fathers (The Thomist Press, Baltimore)[4] had asked her for a contribution on a subject of her own choosing, presumably at the suggestion of Professor Rudolf Allers, who later also translated it into English. This circumstance is important for assessing the writing in view of her overall work; it is likewise a precious biographical record for the time after she fled to the convent in Echt and represents a kind of preparation for her work on St. John of the Cross, *Science of the Cross*, which she began shortly afterwards in 1941. Hence the article was intended for publication from the beginning and was ready for the press in September of 1941, as can be gathered from its imprimatur.

The Archivum Carmelitanum Edith Stein contains the following items under shelf-mark AI 6.

a) A *typewritten copy* with the author's hand corrections and an imprimatur, wrapped in light cardboard with the inscription in the prioress's handwriting "Ways to Know God. 'Symbolic Theology' of the Areopagite and its Objective Presuppositions. I. Copy." 47 sheets, 33.5 x 21.5 cm. Typescript with corrections and additions in Edith Stein's handwriting. We may take this to be the definitive text intended for publication. The typewriter used lacked umlauts [ä, ö, ü] and the digraph ß; the ribbon was spent and the copy paper worn.

b) Two manuscripts prior to the typed copy:

Manuscript I.1. It agrees with the typed version, except for chapter 4c from part II ("Symbolic Theology"). II.4c in this manuscript is entitled "Experiential Knowledge of God," where manuscript I.2 (see below) and the typed copy have the heading "Supernatural Experience of God." 41 sheets, 21.5 x 17 cm. Latin script, ink, most sheets two-sided.

Manuscript I.2. It contains the new chapter II.4c ("Supernatural Experience of God") which tallies with the typed copy. The pagination of the sheets starts where the chapter begins in the typed copy; 6 sheets, 34 x 22 cm., plus one sheet 16 x 21.5 cm. Latin script, ink. Typescript with annotations in Edith Stein's handwriting.

c) A *folder* containing handwritten manuscripts I.1 and I.2 with a censor's comments referring to pages. After these comments is a note in Edith Steins handwriting: "rewrite if necessary 28–34 and p. 41, last sentence p. 20." She carefully followed the censor's comments in the typed copy. Her note "rewrite if necessary 28–34..." refers to the page numbers of section II.4c, obviously typed by someone else in the typewritten version (page changes required by the copy were entered later). Hence we can assume that Edith Stein subsequently altered chapter II.4c of "Ways to Know God."

d) A *carbon copy* of the typed copy with corrections in Edith Stein's hand.

e) *Manuscript II*, a fragment (loose sheets without title page) touching on themes from "Ways to Know God" and treating the first and second ways of the knowledge of God according to the Areopagite. It is a version that obviously precedes manuscripts I.1 and I.2; however, the wording is not the same (We thank Dr. Walter Biemel, former assistant of the Husserl Archives in Louvain, Belgium, and editor of the first volumes of the *Husserliana* series, for his help in the reconstruction of this fragment). 14 sheets, 21.5 x 17 cm. Paging 17–24, 25–36d, 37–38. Latin script, ink, one-sided. The sheets are legible but spotted and blurred by dampness in many places.

f) An *offprint* from *The Thomist* (July, 1946): 379–420 ("Ways to Know God. The 'Symbolic Theology' of Dionysius the Areopagite and its Factual Presuppositions. Translated by Rudolf Allers").

g) An *offprint* from *Tijdschrift voor Philosophie* (February, 1946): 27–74, "Wege der Gotteserkenntnis. Die 'Symbolische Theologie' des Areopagiten und ihre sachlichen Voraussetzungen," published in German for the first time by Lucy Gelber in collaboration with Walter Biemel."

The version of "Ways to Know God" republished in the present volume of Edith Stein's Collected Works is the result of a revision of the original text going back several years. The text here is authoritative wherever it differs from the first edition. It is based on the typewritten version ("a" above) with account taken of all the corrections she entered (mostly alterations related to the censor's comments) and of the new substantially expanded chapter 4c in part II, "Supernatural Experience of God" ("b" above). The fragmentary Manuscript II ("e" above) is appended and published here for the first time.

Manuscript I.1, "Ways to Know God" ("b" above), was written in great outer and inner turmoil, to judge from the page layout, the appearance of the handwriting, and the changes made. In contrast, the newly added chapter II.4c seems to have been composed in great calm. This is also why this study, her last before *Science of the Cross*, is particularly important for throwing light upon her personality. She no doubt experienced the momentary elevation from faith to knowledge. She nowhere mentioned whether she also underwent "mystical experiential knowledge," but it cannot be ruled out. We could take the following points as indications that she did have this experience:

— her express addition (page 32 of the manuscript) that she does not wish to write about it;

— her keen analysis of this state, hardly conceivable without personal experience (manuscript pages 21–33);

— that she belongs to them and presumably includes herself among those "who have already experienced a certain enlightenment and hence are striving for holiness" (manuscript page 55 ["Ways to Know God," 4c4]).

Additional Note on the Text

Titles and subtitles of the writings in this book have been made uniform, spelling and punctuation standardized according to current guidelines, and excessively long sections subdivided. Occasionally missing words are supplied in accord with the sense (such alterations are not indicated in the text).

DR. L. GELBER

I

Husserl and Aquinas: A Comparison

**WHAT IS PHILOSOPHY?
A CONVERSATION
BETWEEN
EDMUND HUSSERL
AND THOMAS AQUINAS**

Dramatis Personae

St. Thomas Aquinas
Edmund Husserl

Scene

The study of
Privy Councilor Husserl
Freiburg

Time

April 8, 1929
late evening

Husserl (*alone*): My good visitors meant well with their kind birthday wishes and I certainly would not have missed a one.

**AN ATTEMPT
TO CONTRAST
HUSSERL'S
PHENOMENOLOGY
AND THE PHILOSOPHY
OF ST. THOMAS AQUINAS**

By Edith Stein (Speyer)

[*Version B continues
on page 6*]

1

Version A

But after such a day it is hard to relax, and I have always been one for a good night's sleep. Actually, after all the chatter I would appreciate a decent conversation on philosophy to get my mind back on track.

(*A knock*) At this late hour? Come in, please.

A Religious (*in white habit and black mantle*): I'm sorry to bother you so late at night, Professor, but I heard what you just said and thought I might still chance a visit. I wanted to speak with you today—just you and I, for I do not take part in social gatherings—but since early morning I have not had the chance to be alone with you until now.

Husserl (*kindly but somewhat at a loss*): You are most welcome, Reverend Father. I've {20} had religious as students before, but to tell the truth I don't remember having any with your particular color-scheme. Could you please help out my poor memory?

The priest (*smiling slightly*): No, I have never sat at your feet. Only from afar have I

Version B

[*Version B continues on page 6*]

Version A

followed with great interest how your philosophy arose and evolved. And some of your students have come and told me about you. I am Thomas Aquinas.

Husserl: Well, this is certainly the biggest surprise of the day. Do sit down. Forgive me if I am unsure how I should act. I would be grateful for some advice.

Thomas: Quite casually, please. Treat me like any other visitor who comes to talk about philosophy. That's why I'm here, you see.

Husserl: Then do come and sit over here in the corner of my old leather sofa. I've had it since I first lectured at the university, but it's quite comfortable and I doubt I'll ever part with it. May I sit right here by you in my old armchair? And now we can begin our discussion. What sort of topic do you have in mind?

But wait, something is troubling me; I must make an awkward confession. When my *Logical Studies* [2] came out—I assume you know the work—my foes in the modern camp

Version B

[*Version B continues on page 6*]

Version A   ## Version B

criticized it saying "why, this is a new scholasticism!" My answer was: "I don't know about scholasticism, but if that's what scholastics wrote, good for them!" (I am really embarrassed to bring this up to you now—but you're smiling with such kindness and understanding, I doubt really that anyone need blush around you.)

Yes, well this is what I was coming to. To this day I have not gotten around to making a thorough study of scholasticism. I do urge my students to study your works, and I am quite pleased when they gain some sound knowledge of them. But in my own case there just was never enough time.

Thomas: Don't worry about it, my dear colleague. I well know and understand perfectly how, given the way you work, you could {21} do nothing else. That's just why I came today. You won't get around to studying the history of philosophy in the coming decades any more than you did in the past. Indeed you already have your hands full completing your own life's work.

On the other hand, I know how important it is for

[*Version B continues on page 6*]

Version A

Version B

you to see clearly how your work relates to other great philosophers. You always had plenty of trouble with young philosophers who could not be made to discover these relations for their doctoral dissertations as they were supposed to, because, hardly out of the nest, all they wanted was to do systematic research on their own and, to your chagrin, they looked down their nose at anything else.

Well, today, when my own philosophy has become, I would almost want to say, all the rage—when after centuries of scorn and neglect, if you yourself want to be taken seriously as a philosopher, you must utter the words "scholasticism" and "Thomas Aquinas" with respect—you are certainly more than ever concerned that our two philosophies be clearly and neatly set forth and differentiated. What could be simpler than for me to say a few words on the matter myself? But only briefly, in broad outline—which is all we can manage in a brief chat at such an ungodly hour.

Husserl: I wish to listen to the Master's words as a respectful disciple. I'm feeling the very

[*Version B continues on page 6*]

| Version A | Version B |

same solemn awe that I did years ago when my professor, Franz Brentano, would address me.

1. PHILOSOPHY AS RIGOROUS SCIENCE

[*Brentano*]

Thomas: Franz Brentano—here we have a connection at once. It is actually not at all easy to find a way from your thought world into mine; your own disciples have always assured me of this. But Brentano does provide a link. After all, you yourself described in your reminiscences how his manner of handling philosophical issues had won you over for philosophy. His way of thinking and teaching {22} told you that philosophy could be more than aesthetic banter and that done properly could meet the highest standards of scientific rigor that you were accustomed to as a mathematician.	For someone coming from the thought world of Edmund Husserl it is not at all easy to find a way into that of St. Thomas. We may perhaps find a link in connection with Franz Brentano. Husserl himself described in his reminiscences how Brentano's manner of handling philosophical issues had won him over for philosophy. Brentano's way of thinking and teaching told him that philosophy could be more than aesthetic banter and that done properly could meet the highest standards of scientific rigor that he was accustomed to as a mathematician.
But where did Brentano get the unrelenting exactness in his reasoning that captivated you and struck you as so novel in philosophy? Where did his crystal-clear concept formation come from? Where else if not his scholastic heritage?	But where did Brentano get the unrelenting exactness in his reasoning that captivated Husserl and struck him as so novel in philosophy? Where did his crystal-clear concept formation come from? Was it not his scholastic heritage?

Version A

For however much he went his own way, the man had been brought up in our school, and its manner of thinking had shaped his mind, not only his but yours. Saying this does not reflect on your originality.

Version B

Brentano {2/316} had been brought up in the austere school of traditional Catholic philosophy and its manner of thinking had shaped his mind. And in Husserl we find something like it in the precision of his thought and in the economy of his language.

[*Philosophia perennis*]

You understand, of course, I do not mean by this that he passed on specific ideas. When people talk as they do about a *philosophia perennis* [perennial philosophy], they usually have a ready-made doctrinal system in mind, and at times, I believe, you have become annoyed when accused of this.

But *philosophia perennis* also means something else: the spirit of genuine philosophy alive in every true philosopher, in anyone who cannot resist an inner need to search out the λόγος [*logos*, mind, reason] of this world, its *ratio* (as I usually translate the word). The born philosopher—the true philosopher indeed *must* be born as a philosopher— brings this spirit with him into the world as *potency*, as I would

Of course we ought not to think this means he passed on specific ideas. When people talk as they do about a *philosophia perennis* [perennial philosophy]. they usually have a ready-made doctrinal system in mind, and this is already quite opposed to the phenomenological way of doing philosophy.

But *philosophia perennis* also means something else: the spirit of genuine philosophy alive in every true philosopher, in anyone who cannot resist an inner need to search out the λόγος [*logos*, mind, reason] of this world, its *ratio* (as Thomas translated the word). The born philosopher brings this spirit with him into the world—as *potency*, in Thomistic terminology. The potency becomes actualized

Version A

call it. The potency becomes actualized when he meets a mature philosopher, a "teacher." This is the way we reach out to one another over the bounds of space and time. *This* is how Plato, Aristotle, and St. Augustine were my teachers (please note well: not only Aristotle, but Plato and Augustine *as well*), and it was quite impossible for me to do my philosophy otherwise than in an ongoing give-and-take with them.

You, too, had your teachers. Some you mentioned explicitly; I recall Descartes, Hume and, again, Brentano. Some influenced you along hidden routes without your being quite aware of it—I am among these.

Version B

when he meets a mature philosopher, a "teacher." This is the way true philosophers reach out to one another over the bounds of space and time. *This* is how Plato, Aristotle, and St. Augustine were St. Thomas's teachers (note well: not only Aristotle, but Plato and Augustine *as well*), and it was quite impossible for him to do his philosophy otherwise than in an ongoing give-and-take with them.

Husserl, too, had teachers in this sense, despite his intellectual independence. Some he mentioned explicitly; his method, for example, he worked out in conscious exchange with Descartes and Hume. Others influenced him along hidden routes, probably without him being quite aware of it—Thomas was numbered among these.

[*Rigorous science*]

We are in full accord, then, on one point: philosophy ought to be done, as you have put it, *as rigorous science.* {23} Now, one should almost dread to utter the phrase, since it has had the misfortune of becoming a fashionable slogan,

We must see Husserl and Thomas in full accord, then, on one point: philosophy ought to be done, as Husserl put it, *as rigorous science.* Now, one should almost dread to utter the phrase, since like so many phenomenological technical

Version A	Version B

misunderstood by detractor and defender alike, each in his own way. We both rightly think here of the analogy with any other science. Our point is simply that philosophy is not feeling and fancy, soaring enthusiasm; it is a matter of the serious, sober inquiry of reason.

We are both convinced that a λόγος is the force behind all that is, and that our understanding can uncover step by step first one aspect of this λόγος, then another, and so on, as long as it moves ahead in accordance with the principle of the most stringent intellectual honor. We were to differ, of course, on how far this procedure of uncovering λόγος could take us.

terms it has had the misfortune of becoming a fashionable slogan, misunderstood by detractor and defender alike, each in his own way. One should not think here of an analogy with any other science. The point is simply that philosophy is not feeling and fancy, soaring enthusiasm, or even personal views—a question of taste as it were; it is a matter of the serious, sober inquiry of reason.

Both Husserl and Thomas were convinced that a λόγος is the force behind all that is, and that our understanding can uncover step by step first one aspect of this λόγος, then another, and so on, as long as it moves ahead {3/317} in accordance with the principle of the most stringent intellectual honor. They differed, of course, on how far this procedure of uncovering λόγος could take them.

·2. NATURAL AND SUPERNATURAL REASON, FAITH AND KNOWLEDGE

[*Reason as such*]

{**Thomas**}: Neither you nor I ever had any doubts about the *power of ratio*. Your first great

Neither Thomas nor Husserl ever had any doubts about the *power of ratio*. Tracking

Version A

achievement was tracking down skepticism in all its modern disguises and bringing it firmly to earth. But for you *ratio* was never more than *natural reason*, while for me the distinction between natural and *supernatural reason* arises at this point.

You are raising your hand defensively, meaning I have misunderstood you. I expected this protest. "Reason" for you lies beyond its division into "natural" and "supernatural." Distinctions like this, you would say, are empirical. You were referring not to the reason of a human being or of a superhuman being, but to *reason as such*, to what must be the case—notwithstanding any empirical distinctions— wherever reason is meaningfully discussed.

Version B

down skepticism in all its modern disguises and bringing it firmly to earth has been extolled as Husserl's great achievement. But for him *ratio* was never more than *natural reason*, while for Thomas the distinction between natural and *supernatural reason* arises at this point.

Now, Husserl might object that "reason" for him lies beyond its division into "natural" and "supernatural." Distinctions like this, he would say, are empirical. But he is not referring to the reason of a human being or of a super- human being, but to *reason as such*, to what must be the case— notwithstanding any empirical distinctions—wherever reason is meaningfully discussed.

[The bounds of reason]

Transcendental criticism in your sense, however, was not my cause. I was always dealing with realities—"naively," as you say. Now, if I take your viewpoint—and why should I not?—I must claim that we can say a great deal indeed about the {24} essence of reason

Transcendental criticism in Husserl's sense, however, was not St. Thomas's cause. He was always dealing with realities—"naively," as Husserl says. Now, if Thomas were alive today and took Husserl's viewpoint—easily imaginable, surely—he would probably

Version A

as such, about the *ratio* of *ratio* [the notion of reason], over and above the different kinds of knowing beings.

Nevertheless this approach does not suffice to set the limits of our knowledge. All we can do, after all, is work with our *own* organs of knowledge; we can no more get free of them than leap over our shadow. If we are granted an insight into the makeup of higher minds, this does not mean that what is accessible to them becomes accessible to us. This fact was never a problem for me.

You proceed as though our reason had no limits in principle. Certainly, its task is endless and knowledge is an unending process. But it heads straight for its goal: the full truth, which as a regulative idea sets the course it is to take. From the perspective of your philosophy there is no other way to the goal.

My view, though, is that this is the way of *natural* reason. Its way is endless, and this implies that it can never reach its goal but only approach it step by step. Another consequence

Version B

claim that we can say a great deal indeed about the essence of reason as such, about the *ratio* of *ratio* [the notion of reason], over and above the different kinds of knowing beings.

Nevertheless this approach does not suffice to set the limits of our knowledge. All we can do, after all, is work with our *own* organs of knowledge; we can no more get free of them than leap over our shadow. If we are granted an insight into the makeup of higher minds, this does not mean that what is accessible to them becomes accessible to us. This fact was never a problem for Thomas.

Phenomenology proceeds as though our reason had no limits in principle. Certainly, it grants that its task is endless and knowledge is an unending process. But it heads straight for its goal: that is, the full truth, which as a regulative idea sets the course it is to take. From the perspective of this philosophy there is no other way to the goal.

St. Thomas's view is also that this is {4/318} the way of *natural* reason. Its way is endless, and this implies that it can never reach its goal but only approach it step by step.

Version A

is that all human philosophy is bound to be fragmentary.

Version B

Another consequence is that all human philosophy is bound to be fragmentary.

[*Communication of divine knowledge*]

Version A

Now comes a big BUT for me. I can never admit that this is the *only* way of knowledge, nor that truth is but an idea that must be actualized in an unending process—and hence never fully. Full Truth *is;* there is a knowledge that embraces truth completely, a knowledge that, rather than unending process, is unending, infinite, fullness at rest. Such is the *divine knowledge.*

Divine knowledge can impart of its fullness to other minds and in fact does so in the measure of their capacity to understand. This communication can come about in several ways. Natural knowledge is but *one* way; it has definite, specifiable limits. But not everything which is beyond our knowledge naturally is altogether inaccessible to our mind in its original [*ursprünglich*] makeup. It is now on the journey of this life, but one day it will reach its goal, our heavenly fatherland. There it will embrace everything that it can grasp (not, however, all depths of divine

Version B

Now comes a big BUT for Thomas. He would never admit that this is the only way of knowledge, nor that truth is but an idea that must be actualized in an unending process—and hence never fully. Full Truth *is;* there is a knowledge that embraces truth completely, a knowledge that, rather than unending process, is unending, infinite, fullness at rest. Such is the *divine knowledge.*

Divine knowledge can impart of its fullness to other minds and in fact does so in the measure of their capacity to understand. This communication can come about in several ways. Natural knowledge is but *one* way; it has definite, specifiable limits. But not everything which is beyond our knowledge naturally is altogether inaccessible to our mind in its original [*ursprünglich*] makeup. It is on the journey of this life for a time, but once reaching its goal, our heavenly fatherland, there it embraces everything that it can grasp (not, however, all depths of divine

Version A	Version B
truth, which God {25} alone grasps fully). Indeed it will see this everything in a single intuition.	truth, which God alone grasps fully). Indeed it will see this everything in a single intuition.

[Faith]

Version A	Version B
Something of what our mind will then see—what it needs in order to avoid straying from its path to the goal—has been imparted to it through revelation. This it grasps in faith, which on our earthly pilgrimage is a second way of gaining knowledge alongside the natural way. At our goal, both what we now know and what we now take on faith, we will know in another way. The possible extent of our knowledge during our pilgrimage on earth is fixed; we cannot shift its boundaries. What we can attain through knowledge and through faith is likewise fixed.	Something of what our mind then sees—what it needs in order to avoid straying from its path to the goal—has already been imparted to it during its existence on earth through revelation. This it grasps in faith, which during our earthly pilgrimage is a second way of gaining knowledge alongside the natural way. At our goal, both what we know *in via* [on our earthly journey] and what we take on faith *in via*, we know in another way. The possible extent of our knowledge during our pilgrimage on earth is fixed; we cannot shift its boundaries. What we can attain through knowledge and through faith is likewise fixed.
As a rule, only that is a matter of faith which is withheld from our earthly knowledge in principle. However, some things are also imparted through revelation which could be known by way of knowledge by only a few people or without sufficient certainty.	As a rule, only that is a matter of faith which is withheld from our earthly knowledge in principle. However, some things are also imparted through revelation which could be known by way of knowledge by only a few people or without sufficient certainty.

Version A   ## Version B

[Religion and modern philosophy]

Husserl: It never occurred to me to contest the right to faith. It (along with other religious acts that may come to mind, for I always left open even the possibility of seeing visions as a source of religious experience) is the proper appeal in religion as are the senses in the area of external experience.

However, this analogy already implies something else: faith is the proper appeal *for religion, but not for philosophy.* The *theory* of faith does not consist of acts of faith any more than the theory of sense experience consists of acts of sense; faith theory is rather rational knowledge that can *bear upon* and *reflect upon* acts of faith as it can upon any other possible acts.

I believe we understand each other's terminology. When I say "rational knowledge" here I do not mean some specific procedure, say, logical inference in contrast to intuition. I mean, quite broadly, knowledge by reason in general; to express it as you

Now, this sort of thinking is quite remote from all modern philosophy. Husserl, it is true, never thought of contesting the right to faith. Faith as he conceived it (along with other religious acts that may come to mind, for he always {5/319} left open even the possibility of seeing visions as a source of religious experience), is the proper appeal in religion as are the senses in the area of external experience.

However, this analogy already implies something else: faith is the proper appeal *for religion, but not for philosophy.* The *theory* of faith does not consist of acts of faith any more than the theory of sense experience consists of acts of sense; faith theory is rather rational knowledge that can *bear upon* and *reflect upon* acts of faith as it can upon any other possible acts.

(To avoid misunderstanding, when I say "rational knowledge" here I do not mean some specific procedure, say, logical inference in contrast to intuition. I mean, quite broadly, knowledge by reason in general, that is, *natural* knowledge by reason

Version A	Version B

Version A: would I should add: *natural* knowledge by reason.

Version B: in accordance with the distinction just drawn. Thomas, too, had to struggle with the ambiguity of *ratio*.)

Thomas: We do understand each other. Nor have I gotten around the double meaning of *ratio*.

[*Faith and philosophy*]

{**Husserl**}: Now, if I must positively insist from the outset that philosophy of religion should be regarded as a matter of reason and not faith, it would appeal to me even less {26} that faith should have anything else in other areas of philosophy. Indeed what you were saying seems to be nothing short of giving faith a deciding vote on crucial questions in the theory of knowledge.

Now, if the modern philosopher positively insists from the outset that philosophy of religion should be regarded as a matter of reason and not faith, it would naturally appeal to him even less that faith should have a say in other areas of philosophy. And obviously, what I just said indeed amounts to giving faith a deciding vote on matters of principle in the theory of knowledge.

Thomas: You are putting your finger on the crucial point. It is not in fact a specifically philosophical issue but one of marking the bounds of natural reason and at the same time the bounds of a philosophy based on purely natural reason. After all, Kant, too, said that before reason can go about its business its limits must be marked off. But it was self-evident to him as well as to all modern philosophy that

Here we meet a decisive point of difference. Faith is not in fact brought in as a specific philosophical issue, but one of marking the bounds of natural reason and at the same time the bounds of a philosophy based on purely natural reason. After all, Kant, too, said that before reason can go about its business its limits must be marked off. But it was self-evident to him as well as to all modern

Version A

natural reason itself, being "autonomous," has the job of setting its own limits. I might ask here whether, to be able to solve the problem, reason would need some Archimedean fulcrum outside itself—and how it could get out there.

Version B

philosophy that natural reason itself, being "autonomous," has the job of setting its own limits. One might ask whether, to be able to solve the problem, reason would need some Archimedean fulcrum outside itself—and how it could get out there.

[*Faith and reason*]

In all events I do not wish to go into this question; I actually never brought it up in my writings since as far as I was concerned the problem *was* solved without any such critical procedure. As long as faith is taken as a feeling or something else "irrational," it is quite understandable why it should be left out of that procedure. If it had meant that for me, I would not give it a say in philosophical issues either.

For philosophy is also a matter of *ratio* for me (in the broad sense that includes natural and supernatural reason). And you gather, of course, from what I was just saying, that I do not take faith to be irrational at all; that is, having nothing to do with truth and falsehood. On the contrary, faith is a way to truth. Indeed, in the first place it is a way to truth*s* —

In all events we need not go into this question here. For Thomas actually never brought it up in his writings since as far as he was concerned the problem *was* solved without any such critical procedure. As long as faith is taken as a feeling or something else "irrational," it is quite conceivable why it should be left out of that procedure. Had it meant that for Thomas, he would not have given it a say in philosophical issues either.

For philosophy {6/320} is also a matter of *ratio* for Thomas (in the broad sense that includes natural and supernatural reason). And it follows from what I said above that he does not take faith to be irrational at all; that is, having nothing to do with truth and falsehood. On the contrary, faith is a way to truth. Indeed, in the first place it is a way to truth*s* — plural—which would otherwise

Version A

plural—which would otherwise be closed to us, and in the second place it is the *surest* way to truth. For there is no greater certainty than that of faith; what is more, for human beings *in statu viae* [in the state of being on our earthly journey] no knowledge lends a certainty that can come up to that proper to faith, albeit the certainty of faith lacks the obviousness of insight [*uneinsichtig*]. Thus faith is relevant for philosophy in two ways.

Version B

be closed to us, and in the second place it is the *surest* way to truth. For there is no greater certainty than that of faith; what is more, for human beings *in statu viae* [in the state of being on our earthly journey] no knowledge lends a certainty that can come up to that proper to faith, albeit the certainty of faith lacks the obviousness of insight [*uneinsichtig*]. Thus faith is relevant for philosophy in two ways.

[Dependence of philosophy on faith]

Philosophy aspires after truth to the greatest possible extent and with the greatest possible certainty. If faith makes accessible {27} truths unattainable by any other means, philosophy, for one thing, cannot forego them without renouncing its universal claim to truth. Furthermore, it cannot forego these truths without risking that falsehood will creep even into the body of knowledge left to it, since, given the organic interrelationship of all truth, any partial stock, when its link to the whole is cut off, can appear in a false light. One consequence, then, is a *material dependence of philosophy on faith*.

Philosophy aspires after truth to the greatest possible extent and with the greatest possible certainty. If faith makes accessible truths unattainable by any other means, philosophy, for one thing, cannot forego them without renouncing its universal claim to truth. Furthermore, it cannot forego these truths without risking that falsehood will creep even into the body of knowledge left to it, since, given the organic interrelationship of all truth, any partial stock, when its link to the whole is cut off, can appear in a false light. One consequence, then, is a *material dependence of philosophy on faith*.

Version A

Then too, if faith affords the highest certainty attainable by the human mind, and if philosophy claims to bestow the highest certainty, then philosophy must make the certainty of faith its own. It does so first by absorbing the truths of faith, and further by using them as the final criterion by which to gauge all other truths. Hence, a second consequence is a *formal dependence of philosophy on faith*.

Version B

Then too, if faith affords the highest certainty attainable by the human mind, and if philosophy claims to bestow the highest certainty, then philosophy must make the certainty of faith its own. It does so first by absorbing the truths of faith, and further by using them as the final criterion by which to gauge all other truths. Hence, a second consequence is a *formal dependence of philosophy on faith*.

[*Supernatural reason in philosophy*]

Version A

You will have noticed that in my comments I have used the word "philosophy" in two senses, parallel to the above distinction between natural and supernatural reason. We could go ahead and speak of natural and supernatural philosophy, since, after all, it is also customary to divide theology into natural and supernatural components.

There is a body of truths accessible to natural reason. Natural reason no longer suffices by itself to mark its own limits; for this supernatural reason must step in (the way they mesh together should be discussed further). It is also the task of supernatural

Version B

It will be noticed that in my comments I have used the word "philosophy" in two senses, parallel to the above distinction between natural and supernatural reason. We could go ahead and speak of natural and supernatural philosophy, since, after all, it is also customary to divide theology into natural and supernatural components.

There is a body of truths accessible to natural reason. Natural reason no longer suffices by itself to mark its own limits; for this supernatural reason must step in (the way they mesh together should be discussed further). It is also the task of supernatural

Version A	Version B
reason to assess particular truths gained through natural reason.	reason to assess particular truths gained through natural reason.

reason to assess particular truths gained through natural reason.

Besides its methodological service, which consists essentially in keeping natural reason from error, supernatural reason has the material task of supplementing the truths of natural reason. A rational understanding of the world, that is, a metaphysics—in the end, surely, the intention, tacit or overt, of all philosophy—can be {28} gained only by natural and supernatural reason working together. (The loss of the appreciation for this fact accounts for the abstruse character of all modern philosophy and at the same time, quite consistently, for the mistrust of metaphysics felt by so many modern thinkers.)

Natural reason in turn has the task of analyzing the truths of faith and putting them to use [*Auswertung*], of course still under the methodological guidance of supernatural reason. We need not think of this guidance as a constant explicit assessing and comparing. As a rule, natural reason enlightened by faith goes it own way in harmony with supernatural truth, and testing is called for only in borderline cases.

Besides {7/321} its methodological service, which consists essentially in keeping natural reason from error, supernatural reason has the material task of supplementing the truths of natural reason. A rational understanding of the world, that is, a metaphysics—in the end, surely, the intention, tacit or overt, of all philosophy—can be gained only by natural and supernatural reason working together. (The loss of the appreciation for this fact accounts for the abstruse character of all modern metaphysics and at the same time, quite consistently, for the mistrust of metaphysics felt by so many modern thinkers.)

Natural reason in turn has the task of analyzing the truths of faith and putting them to use [*Auswertung*], of course still under the methodological guidance of supernatural reason. We need not think of this guidance as a constant explicit assessing and comparing. As a rule, natural reason enlightened by faith goes it own way in harmony with supernatural truth, and testing is called for only in borderline cases.

Version A

I should add, by the way, that you will find scarcely anything of what I have just been saying about the relation of faith and reason in my writings. For me it was all a self-evident starting point. I am speaking now from a later reflection on how I actually proceed, as it is needed today for a rapprochement with moderns.

Version B

I should add here that scarcely anything of what I have just been saying about the relation of faith and reason is to be found in St. Thomas's writings. For him it was all a self-evident starting point. The comments I have ventured to make are based upon a later reflection on how he actually proceeds, as it is needed today for a rapprochement with moderns.

[*The warrant of faith*]

Husserl: Getting used to these ways of thinking demands from me such a complete re-adjustment, that at the moment I would not like to say anything about them. I would only like to ask one question: if faith is the final criterion of all other truth, what is the criterion of faith itself? What guarantees that the certainty of my faith is genuine?

At this point the "critically" inclined contemporary philosopher will feel bound to ask: if faith is the last criterion of all other truth, what is the criterion of faith itself? What guarantees that the certainty of my faith is genuine?

Thomas: It goes without saying that you must ask this question. Probably my best answer is that faith is its own guarantee.

I could also say that God, who has given us the revelation, vouches for its truth. But this would only be the other side of the same coin. For if we took the two as separate

Probably the best answer according to the mind of St. Thomas is that faith is its own guarantee.

We could also say that God, who has given us the revelation, vouches for its truth. But this would only be the other side of the same coin. For if we took the two as separate

Version A

facts, we would fall into a *circulus vitiosus* [vicious circle], since God is after all what we become certain about in faith.

Nor would it help to appeal to arguments for God's existence, for since they involve natural knowledge, through them we can gain only the certitude of natural knowledge, not that peculiar to faith.

Version B

facts, we would fall into a *circulus vitiosus* [vicious circle], since the God who is presented to us in revelation and who is personally close to us, is after all what we become certain about in faith.

Nor would it help to appeal to arguments for God's existence. To be sure, the understanding has ways to demonstrate the existence of God by ascending from creatures and also to gain—even if only negatively and analogically— a certain image of the divine essence. But since these *praeambula fidei* [preambles of the faith] involve natural knowledge, through them we can gain {8/322} only the certitude of natural knowledge, not that peculiar to faith.

[Faith as gift]

All we can do is point out that for the believer such is the certainty of faith that it relativizes all other certainty, and that he can but give up any supposed knowledge which contradicts his faith. The {29} unique certitude of faith is a gift of grace. It is up to the understanding and will to draw the theoretical and

All we can do is point out that for the believer such is the certainty of faith that it relativizes all other certainty, and that he can but give up any supposed knowledge which contradicts his faith. The unique certitude of faith is a gift of grace. It is up to the understanding and will to draw the theoretical and

Version A	Version B
practical consequences therefrom. Constructing a philosophy on faith belongs to the theoretical consequences.	practical consequences therefrom. Constructing a philosophy on faith belongs to the theoretical consequences.

3. CRITICAL AND DOGMATIC PHILOSOPHY

[*Starting points*]

{**Thomas**}: You see that the basic position of a philosopher setting out from such a position must differ entirely from that of the modern philosopher who excludes faith and would make do with natural knowledge alone. We *have* from the outset the absolute certainty we need to build a sound edifice; you modern philosophers must first search for some such starting point. So it is quite clear why the critique of knowledge was bound to become the fundamental area of modern philosophy and why its great representatives had to devote their main efforts to it.	Obviously, the basic position of a philosopher setting out from such a position must differ entirely from that of the modern philosopher who excludes faith and would make do with natural knowledge alone. The philosopher who stands on the ground of faith *has* from the outset the absolute certainty he needs to build a sound edifice; others must first search for some such starting point. So it is quite clear why the critique of knowledge was bound to become the fundamental area of modern philosophy and why its great representatives had to devote their main efforts to it.

[*Husserl's quest for security*]

This has also been true with you. You began with specific problems but were forced back step by step in an effort to secure an absolutely reliable method.	This has also been true with Husserl. He began with specific problems but was forced back step by step in an effort to secure an absolutely reliable method.

Version A

You sought to eliminate all possible sources of error. You did away with fallacies in reasoning by renouncing all conclusions reached through mediate thinking and by allowing use of immediately evident states of affairs only. The deception of the senses you avoided by setting aside natural experience and by developing a method of pure inquiry into essence.

By extending Descartes' methodic doubt and ridding Kant's critique of reason of its uncritical elements, you came to define the sphere of the transcendentally purified consciousness as the field of inquiry for his *prima philosophia* [first philosophy] (in your sense).

But even here you could not rest. You uncovered traces of transcendence even in this sphere, and until today you have been making efforts to stake out within it a realm of genuine immanence—that is to say, a knowledge that is absolutely one with its object and hence safe from all doubt.

It is surely clear to you by now that I do not think {30} this goal is attainable. The ideal of knowledge, as I have just described it, is realized in God's knowledge; for him

Version B

His method sought to eliminate all possible sources of error. It did away with fallacies in reasoning by renouncing all conclusions reached through mediate thinking and by allowing use of immediately evident states of affairs only. The deception of the senses it avoided by setting aside natural experience and by establishing itself as a method of pure inquiry into essence.

By extending Descartes' methodic doubt and ridding Kant's critique of reason of its uncritical elements, Husserl came to define the sphere of the transcendentally purified consciousness as the field of inquiry for his *prima philosophia* [first philosophy].

But even here there was no stopping. Traces of transcendence showed up even in this sphere, and in recent years his efforts have been to stake out within it a realm of genuine immanence—that is to say, a knowledge that would be absolutely one with its object and hence safe from all doubt.

It is surely clear by now that from St. Thomas's point of view this goal is unattainable {9/323}. The ideal of knowledge as it was just described is realized in God's knowledge;

Version A	Version B
being and knowing are one, but for us they are separate.	for him being and knowing are one, but for us they are separate.

[*Knowledge in Thomas*]

Therefore you need not think your critical procedure is pointless for me. By no means. It made it possible to sort out and order the means to knowledge and—as long as it is applied with the same radical rigor as you did—to gain a methodological purity perhaps unknown before.	Nonetheless, we need not think that this critical procedure would be pointless for Thomas. By no means. We may acknowledge from his standpoint that Husserl's procedure made it possible to sort out and order the means to knowledge and—as long as it is applied with the same radical rigor as did Husserl himself—to gain a methodological purity perhaps unknown before.
My philosophy also accommodates a theory of knowledge in this sense of ordering and sifting the means of knowing. But for me it was and could be a *cura posterior* [secondary issue]. In the calm assurance that I could avail myself of a series of lawful ways of acquiring knowledge, I felt free to use all of them to gather the greatest possible wealth of philosophical knowledge. What mattered to me was the *what*, not the *how*. You call that procedure "dogmatic." I welcomed any way as long as it led to the truth. I could	St. Thomas's philosophy would also accommodate a theory of knowledge in this sense of ordering and sifting the means of knowing. But for him it was and could be a *cura posterior* [secondary issue]. In the calm assurance that he could avail himself of a series of lawful ways of acquiring knowledge, he felt free to use all of them to gather the greatest possible wealth of philosophical knowledge. What mattered to him was the *what*, not the *how*. Phenomenology calls that procedure "dogmatic." Thomas's spirit of

Version A	Version B
leave the discussion of knowledge issues to wherever they happened to come up in the order of the questions I was treating.	synthesis welcomed any way as long as it led to the truth. He could leave the discussion of knowledge issues to wherever they happened to come up in the order of the questions he was treating.

[Thomas's accomplishment]

I had to do what was needed for my time. An abundance of hitherto unknown knowledge had been brought to me. Exciting questions were being asked: *may* we assimilate some of this knowledge and *what* may we assimilate? The only way to serve the cause of truth and people's peace of mind was to gather up the whole stock of the knowledge of my time and put it to the test.	Thomas himself had to do what was needed for his time. An abundance of hitherto unknown knowledge had been brought to his age. Exciting questions were being asked: *may* we assimilate some of this knowledge and *what* may we assimilate? The only way to serve the cause of truth and people's peace of mind was to gather up the whole stock of knowledge of the time and put it to the test.
I could not dwell over preliminary inquiries which from my point of view and for my purpose were unnecessary; if I had, I would not have been able to accomplish my mission. I brought together doctrines of the church, Holy Scripture and the Fathers, as well as teachings of philosophies, ancient and recent. I ordered, compared, and tested. And I used all appropriate means in testing: the principles of formal	Thomas could not dwell over preliminary inquiries which from his point of view and for his purpose were unnecessary; if he had, he would not have been able to accomplish his mission. He brought together doctrines of the church, Holy Scripture and the Fathers, as well as teachings of philosophers, ancient and recent. He ordered, compared, and tested. And he used all appropriate means in testing: the principles of formal

Version A

logic, objective insight, assessment by the truth of faith.

A cursory inspection of my writings might give the impression that human authority was also an important criterion for me. But the impression is deceptive. Certainly, it carried great weight for me when Aristotle {31}—whom I called "*the* Philosopher" *par excellence*—or Augustine endorsed some position. I was always convinced that their words must contain a grain of truth. Nor was I adverse to quoting them as a key *argumentum ad hominem* [personal criticism] against others. But never did I accept on purely human authority anything accessible at all to my own insight.

Version B

logic, objective insight, assessment by the truth of faith.

A cursory inspection of his writings might give the impression that human authority was also an important criterion for Thomas. But the appearance is deceptive. Certainly, it carried great weight for him when Aristotle—whom he called "*the* Philosopher" *par excellence*—or Augustine endorsed some position. He was always convinced that their words must contain a grain of truth. Nor {10/324} was he adverse to quoting them as a key *argumentum ad hominem* [personal criticism] against others. But never did he accept on purely human authority anything accessible to his own insight.

[*Thomas's "system"*]

What has been called my "system" took shape in this work of assembling, sifting, ordering. The body of knowledge of my time became organized in my mind. I wrote no "philosophical system," nor has the system behind my works been written so far.

Yet anyone who studies my works will find clear, definite answers, perhaps to more questions than he himself

What has been called St. Thomas's "system" took shape in this work of assembling, sifting, ordering. The body of knowledge of his time became organized in his mind. He wrote no "philosophical system," nor has the system behind his works been written so far.

Yet anyone who studies his works will find clear, definite answers, perhaps to more questions than he himself

Version A	Version B
could ask. And what is more, the *organon* [systematic principles for acquiring knowledge] that I bore within myself and that enabled me to settle a host of issues with a firm, serene *respondeo dicendum* [in reply it ought to be said that], leaves its mark on my "disciple" and gives him the ability to answer questions in my spirit that I never asked and possibly at the time could not have been asked at all.	could ask. And what is more, the *organon* [systematic principles for acquiring knowledge] that the Master bore within himself and that enabled him to settle a host of issues with a firm, serene *respondeo dicendum* [in reply it ought to be said that], leaves its mark on his "disciple" and gives him the ability to answer questions in Thomas's spirit that Thomas never asked and possibly at the time could not have been asked at all.

[*A philosophy to be lived*]

This may well also be the reason why folks today are coming back to my works. Ours is a time that is no longer content with methodical deliberations. People have nothing to hold on to and are looking for purchase. They want a truth to cling to, a meaning for their lives; they want a "philosophy for life." And this they find in me.	This may well also be the reason why folks today are going back to his writings. Ours is a time that is no longer content with methodical deliberations. People have nothing to hold on to and are looking for purchase. They want a truth to cling to, a meaning for their lives; they want a "philosophy for life." And this they find in Thomas.
Of course there is a world of difference between my philosophy and what passes for "philosophy for life" today. In my philosophy you will look in vain for flights of emotion; all you will find is truth, soberly grasped in abstract concepts. On the surface much of it looks like theoretical "hair-splitting" that you cannot "do"	Of course there is a world of difference between Thomas's philosophy and what passes for "philosophy for life" today. In his philosophy we will look in vain for flights of emotion; all we will find is truth, soberly grasped in abstract concepts. On the surface much of it looks like theoretical "hair-splitting" that we cannot "do"

Version A

anything with. And even after serious study it is not easy to put your finger on practical returns.

But if someone has lived with me for some time, dwelt in my intellectual world, he will come to feel more and more that he is making right choices with ease and confidence on difficult theoretical issues or in practical situations where before he would have been helpless. And {32} if later he thinks back—even surprising himself—on how he managed it, he will realize that a bit of Thomas's "hairsplitting" laid the groundwork. At the time that I was working on this or that problem, I naturally had no idea what it could some day be "good for," nor was I concerned about it. I was but following out the law of truth; truth bears fruit of itself.

Version B

anything with. And even after serious study it is not easy to put our finger on practical returns.

But a person who has lived for some time with the mind of St. Thomas—lucid, keen, calm, cautious—and dwelt in his world, will come to feel more and more that he is making right choices with ease and confidence on difficult theoretical issues or in practical situations where before he would have been helpless. And if later he thinks back— even surprising himself—on how he managed it, he will realize that a bit of Thomas's "hairsplitting" laid the ground-work. At the time that Thomas was working on this or that problem, he naturally had no idea what it could some day be "good for," nor was he concerned about it. He was but following out the law of truth; truth bears fruit of itself. {11/325}

4. THEOCENTRIC AND EGOCENTRIC PHILOSOPHY

[*First truth*]

{**Thomas**}: Our different goals and different conceptions of the basis of certainty were bound to give a completely

Different goals and different conceptions of the basis of certainty were bound to give a completely different thrust to

Version A | ## Version B

Version A	Version B
different thrust to each philosophy as a whole. Both of us set out from the premise that objective existence [*Bestehen*] belongs to the notion of truth, independently of the person seeking or knowing it at a time. But on the issue of *first* truth, and with it of first philosophy, our ways part company.	each philosophy as a whole. Both of them set out from the premise that objective existence [*Bestehen*] belongs to the notion of truth, independently of the person seeking or knowing it at a time. But on the issue of *first* truth, and with it of first philosophy, their ways part company.

[Thomas's ontology]

For me, the first axiom of philosophy—if you wish to use the word—is that God himself is the first Truth, the principle and criterion of all truth. From him proceeds any truth we can get hold of. The task of first philosophy follows from this fact: it must take God as its object. It must set forth the idea of God and the meaning of his being; moreover, the relationship to God of whatever else that exists, in its essence and existence, and the relationship to the divine knowledge of the knowledge of other knowing beings. We must bring to bear on these questions *everything* we can know about them, taking what we should not only from natural knowledge but also from revelation. In regard to the knowledge of creatures, we must also discuss the ways in	For Thomas, the first axiom of philosophy—if we wish to use the word—is that God himself is the first Truth, the principle and criterion of all truth. From God proceeds any truth we can get hold of. The task of first philosophy follows from this fact: it must take God as its object. It must set forth the idea of God and the mode of his being and knowing. Then it must establish the relationship to God of whatever else that exists, in its essence and existence, and the relationship to the divine knowledge of the knowledge of other knowing beings. We must bring to bear on these questions *everything* we can know about them, taking what we should not only from natural knowledge but also from revelation. In regard to the knowledge of creatures, we

Version A

which creatures having our psychological makeup can come to know God, themselves, and other creatures.

Thus the theory of knowledge, which you [moderns] place at the outset to "justify" all that follows, turns out to form part of a general theory of being. Thus all questions at bottom come down to questions about being, and {33} all areas of philosophy become parts of a great ontology or metaphysics. For God imparts to every being [*Wesen*] *what* it is and the manner of its being, its essence and existence, but he also imparts to it, in accordance with its essence and existence, the extent and manner of its knowing and striving, the truth and perfection which it can attain.

In this way logic, knowledge theory, and ethics, as far as their material content is concerned, are contained within ontology—although they may also be constructed in another way, given a normative turn, as disciplines in their own right.

Version B

must discuss the ways in which creatures having our psychological makeup can come to know God, themselves, and other creatures.

Thus the theory of knowledge, which moderns place at the outset to "justify" all that follows, turns out to form part of a general theory of being. Thus all questions at bottom come down to questions about being, and all areas of philosophy become parts of a great ontology or metaphysics. For God imparts to every being *what* it is and the manner of its being [*Wesen*], its essence and existence, but he also imparts to it, in accordance with its essence and existence, the extent and manner of its knowing and striving, the truth and perfection which it can attain.[3]

In this way logic, knowledge theory, and ethics, as far as their material content is concerned, are contained within ontology—although they may also be constructed in another way, given a normative turn, as disciplines in their own right.

[Phenomenology and Thomistic ontology]

You surely see too how "transcendental phenomenology," your most distinctive creation, fits into this *organon:* it

It is evident how Husserl's "transcendental phenomenology," his most distinctive creation, fits {12/326} into this *organon:*

Version A

is this general ontology, with a radical shift of sign (to use your own expression) since it corresponds to your differing basic position.

The question for you is this: How is the world constructed for a consciousness that I can explore in immanence: the inner and outer world, the world of nature and mind, the value-free world and the world of goods, and ultimately the world charged with religious meaning, the world of God?

You have been tireless in your efforts to perfect a method that would allow you to pursue these "constitutive" issues and show how the intellectual activity of the subject, working on the pure material of sensation, constructs his "world" through various acts and assemblages of acts.

My general ontology, which assigns a specific activity to every being possessed of mind, surely accommodates these constitutive investigations. But it cannot concede a "fundamental" significance to them.

Version B

it *is* this general ontology, with a radical shift of sign (to use Husserl's own expression), corresponding as it does to his differing basic position.

The question for the transcendental approach is this: How is the world constructed for a consciousness that I can explore in immanence: the inner and outer world, the world of nature and mind, the value-free world and the world of goods, and ultimately the world charged with religious meaning, the world of God?

Husserl has been tireless in his efforts to perfect a method that would allow him and his students to pursue these "constitutive" issues and show how the intellectual activity of the subject, working on the pure material of sensation, constructs his "world" through various acts and assemblages of acts.

Thomas's general ontology, which assigns a specific activity to every being possessed of mind, surely accommodates these constitutive investigations. But it cannot concede a "fundamental" significance to them.

[*Husserl and Catholic philosophy*]

The course that you followed has led you to posit the

The course that transcendental phenomenology

Version A

subject as the start and center of philosophical inquiry; all else is subject-related. A world constructed by the acts of the subject remains forever a world for the subject. You could not succeed—and this was the constant objection that your own students raised against you—in winning back from the realm of immanence *that* objectivity from which you had after all set out and insuring which was the point. Once existence is redefined as self-identifying for a consciousness—such was the outcome of the transcendental investigation—the intellect will never be set at ease in its search for truth.

Moreover, this shift in meaning, especially by relativizing God himself, contradicts {34} faith. So here we may well have the sharpest contrast between transcendental phenomenology and my philosophy: mine has a *theocentric* and yours an *egocentric* orientation.

Version B

followed has led it to posit the subject as the start and center of philosophical inquiry; all else is subject-related. A world constructed by the acts of the subject remains forever a world for the subject. Phenomenology could not succeed on such a course—and this was the constant objection that his own students raised against its Founder—in winning back from the realm of immanence *that* objectivity from which he had after all set out and insuring which was the point: a truth and reality free from any relatedness to the subject. Once existence is redefined as self-identifying for a consciousness—such was the outcome of the transcendental investigation—the intellect searching for truth will never be set at ease.

Moreover, this shift in the meaning, especially by relativizing God himself, contradicts faith. So here we may well have the sharpest contrast between transcendental phenomenology and Catholic philosophy: the latter has a *theocentric* and the former an *egocentric* orientation.

[Husserl's idealism]

Husserl: I do not wish to enter into a discussion of this. It was

It was in fact chiefly his much talked-about "idealism"

Version A

indeed this point, my much talked-about "idealism," that was criticized in the years following the appearance of my *Ideas*,[4] wherein it was first expressed. I have gone over it often enough with my zealous students, and I must confess to you that arguments that for me were conclusive proved more often than not unable to convince my opponents in these discussions, and even when one of them gave up for the moment, sooner or later he would come back with the old objections or perhaps new ones as well.

This is also why in recent years I have striven over and over to deepen and hone the analyses that led me to this position. And now I am still seeking a cogent way to state the connections that would make its coherence as lucid for others as I feel it is for myself.

You see, I do not admit defeat. But today I am your student, not a professor. So now I would like to ask for information on still another point.

Version B

that was criticized in the years following the appearance of his *Ideas*,[4] wherein it was first expressed. It was just this issue that his zealous students kept bringing up in their discussions with him without ever reaching any conclusion. Arguments that for Husserl were conclusive, proved more often than not unable to convince his opponents in these discussions, and even when one of them gave up for the moment, sooner or later he would come back {13/327} with the old objections or perhaps new ones as well.

So it is that Husserl in recent years has felt obliged to devote all his energy to deepen and hone the analyses that led him to this position and find a cogent way to state the connections that would make its coherence as lucid for others as he feels it is for himself. On this issue, then, the course of phenomenology has diverged more and more from that of medieval philosophy.

Version A   Version B

5. ONTOLOGY AND METAPHYSICS, EMPIRICAL AND EIDETIC METHODS

[Essence and fact]

{**Husserl**}: You spoke of ontology *or* metaphysics. I am used to keeping the two terms apart. I wished to establish as sciences of essence—those making no use of empirical findings—what I called formal and a material ontology: disciplines presupposed to all activity of the positive sciences, such as pure logic, pure mathematics, the pure natural sciences, etc.

Now metaphysics in your traditional sense, on the other hand, seems to me to be essentially a science of *this* world. How do you view this distinction between *essence* and *fact*, between *eidetics* and *empirics*?

Thomas: I did not distinguish them as a matter of methodological principle as sharply {35} as you did. As you quite rightly said, and as I have stressed before, I was after the broadest possible picture of *this* world. (By "*this* world," incidentally, you mean the factually existing world as distinct from any possible

I spoke just now of ontology *or* metaphysics. Phenomenologists usually keep the two terms apart. Husserl wished to found as sciences of essence—those making no use of empirical findings—what he calls formal and a material ontology: disciplines presupposed to all activity of the positive sciences, such as pure logic, pure mathematics, the pure natural sciences, etc.

On the other hand, metaphysics in the traditional sense seems in contrast to be essentially a science of *this* world. Thomas does not in fact distinguish as a matter of methodological principle as sharply as phenomenology would expect between *essence* and *fact*, between eidetics and empirics.

I have already stressed that Thomas was after the broadest possible picture of *this* world. (By "*this* world," incidentally, Husserl means the factually existing world as distinct from any possible

Version A	Version B
world, not the earthly world as distinct from the world above).	world, not the earthly world as distinct from the world above).

[*Theory and practice*]

Version A	Version B
For philosophers in the Middle Ages, after all, philosophy was never a purely theoretical affair, even when like myself they were working as pure theoreticians. They were rather seeking an understanding of the world as a basis for correct practical behavior in the world. This was not their sole or even their highest motive for doing philosophy, but it was still important (I know, by the way, that this motive is never far from your thoughts). For medieval philosophers fully recognized the claims of pure theory; indeed, it is by knowing truth that the intellect fulfills the meaning of its existence and attains its greatest possible likeness to God as his image and its supreme happiness.	For philosophers in the Middle Ages, after all, philosophy was never a purely theoretical affair, even when like Thomas they were working as pure theoreticians. They were rather seeking an understanding of the world as a basis for correct practical behavior in the world. This was not their sole or even their highest motive for doing philosophy, but it was still important (it has also, by the way, always been an important motive for Husserl). For medieval philosophers fully recognized the claims of pure theory; indeed, it is by knowing truth that the intellect fulfills the meaning of its existence and attains its greatest possible likeness to God and its supreme happiness.
Both empirical and eidetic knowledge were needed for this practical goal as well as for the theoretical goal of acquiring the broadest possible knowledge [*Kenntnis*] of the world. Faith's contribution to this world view is indeed largely knowledge of facts, even though knowing [*Wissen*]	Both empirical and eidetic knowledge were needed for this practical goal as well as for the theoretical goal of acquiring the broadest possible knowledge [*Kenntnis*] of the world. Faith's contribution to this world view is indeed largely knowledge of facts {14/328}, even though knowing [*Wissen*]

Version A

by faith is of a valence different from that based on sense experience.

Version B

by faith is of a valence different from that based on sense experience.

[*Essence and accident*]

Version A

At the same time I was thoroughly familiar with the distinction. I spoke about what applies to things "in themselves," according to their "essence"—"essentially," as you say—and about what applies to them "accidentally," owing to the combination of circumstances they have gotten into in the practical course of events.

I laid my chief emphasis on essential truths. In fact, what applies to things according to their essence is as it were the basic scaffolding of the world. And what befalls them accidentally is already provided for in their essence as possibility.

In this sense you, too, have indeed brought the factual into your reflections on essence. Hence to a large extent your inquiry and mine share a common approach—you would be surprised how much our particular analyses often follow the same method. And your opponents were quite right in spotting this similarity

Version B

At the same time the medieval philosopher was thoroughly familiar with the distinction. He speaks about what applies to things "in themselves," according to their "essence"—"essentially," as phenomenologists say—and about what applies to them "accidentally," owing to the combination of circumstances they have gotten into in the factual course of events.

He lays his chief emphasis on essential truths. In fact, what applies to things according to their essence is as it were the basic scaffolding of the world. And what befalls them accidentally is already provided for in their essence as possibility.

In this sense Husserl, too, has indeed brought the factual into his reflections on essence. Hence to a large extent phenomenological and scholastic inquiry share a common approach—it is often surprising how much their particular analyses follow the same method. And the opponents of phenomenology were quite

Version A	Version B
when they labeled your method a renewal of scholasticism. {36}	right in spotting this similarity when they labeled the method of essence analysis followed in Husserl's *Logical Studies*[2] a renewal of scholasticism.

[*Possibility and actuality*]

Version A	Version B
On the other hand the fact remains that I was concerned to highlight the essence of *this* world and all the things of this world, and hence that what you usually call the existence-claim always remained intact. A play of free possibilities was not my concern. My remarks on the knowledge of angels, the knowledge of the first human being, the knowledge of the soul after death, etc., are statements about reality. They are not meant merely to suggest *possible* kinds of knowledge alongside kinds of factual human knowledge based on experience, thus attaining a breadth of knowledge as such that subsumes its varieties. Your students granted this meaning to scholastic inquiries, and their work on such possibility issues, of which they were especially fond, gave them access to our thought world—whereas other currents of modern philosophy could make nothing of it at all.	On the other hand the fact remains that Thomas was concerned to highlight the essence of *this* world and all the things of this world and hence that what Husserl usually calls the existence-claim always remained intact. A play of free possibilities was not his concern. His remarks on the knowledge of angels, the knowledge of the first human being, the knowledge of the soul after death, etc., are statements about reality. They are not meant merely to suggest *possible* kinds of knowledge alongside kinds of factual human knowledge based on experience, thus attaining a breadth of knowledge as such that subsumes its varieties. Phenomenologists granted this meaning to scholastic inquiries, and their work on such possibility issues, of which they were especially fond, gave them access to the thought world of the Middle Ages—whereas other currents of modern philosophy could make nothing of it at all.

Version A	Version B

[Thomas and phenomenology]

| Both senses *are present* in my writings, and we could follow up each one by itself, bringing together and expounding separately what belongs to "ontology" and to "metaphysics." Then we would have to combine what is already present in your works and in those of your students to meet your demand for a formal ontology and for a series of material ontologies. | Both senses *are present* in St. Thomas's writings, and we could follow up each one by itself, sorting out and expounding separately what belongs to "ontology" and what to "metaphysics." Then we would have to classify what is already contained {15/329} in the works of Husserl and his students to meet his demand for a formal ontology and for a series of material ontologies. |
| It would then emerge how far there is an agreement. No proper contrast can be made as long as we speak only in general way of "essence" opposed to fact and of the "in itself" opposed to the accidental, since these general expressions are hardly more than shorthand for an array of difficult ontological problems. | It would then emerge how far there is an agreement. No proper contrast can be made as long as we speak only in general way of "essence" opposed to fact and of the "in itself" opposed to the accidental, since these general expressions are hardly more than shorthand for an array of difficult ontological problems. |

6. THE "INTUITION" QUESTION— PHENOMENOLOGICAL AND SCHOLASTIC METHODS

[Methods and misunderstandings]

| {Thomas}: In this connection we would run into another question that outsiders might have {37} expected to be the first thing to come up in a conversation between us: the | In this connection we would run into another question that outsiders may take to be the most important for contrasting Thomas and Husserl: the much discussed |

Version A

much discussed question of *intuition* or *essence-viewing.* It may well have been the greatest stumbling block in your philosophy for Kantians and neo-scholastics.

It is quite understandable why phenomenological and scholastic methods gave a superficial impression of being basically at odds. The scholastic method (if we speak only of natural knowledge) involves the logical processing and exploiting [*Auswertung*] of sense experience. The phenomenological method is supposed to be an immediate beholding of eternal truths, which in scholasticism is reserved for pure spirits. Now, if we think this is all there is to it, I must say we have done both of us a disservice.

To begin with, the words "intuition" [*Intuition*] and "viewing" [*Erschauen*] have caused trouble. They do in fact come burdened with a history, and someone up on mystical literature was sure to imagine something like an intellectual vision, a preview of the *visio beatifica* [beatific vision]. Such visions are a privilege of chosen souls, ordinarily

Version B

question of *intuition* or *essence-viewing.* It may well have been the greatest stumbling block in phenomenology for materialists and positivists, Kantians and neo-scholastics alike.

It is quite understandable why phenomenological and scholastic methods gave a superficial impression of being basically at odds. The scholastic method (if we speak only of natural knowledge) involves the logical processing and exploiting [*Auswertung*] of sense experience. The phenomenological method is supposed to be an immediate beholding of eternal truths, which in Scholasticism is reserved for the blessed spirits, and indeed, if we take "immediate" in the strict sense, for God himself. Now, if we think this is all there is to it, we must say we have done both approaches a disservice.

To begin with, the words "intuition [*Intuition*] and "viewing" [*Erschauen*] have caused trouble. They do in fact come burdened with a history, and someone up on mystical literature was sure to imagine something like an intellectual vision, a preview of the *visio beatifica* [beatific vision]. Such visions are a privilege of chosen souls, ordinarily

Version A

those prepared for it by a high degree of holiness and austerity of life, although even the greatest holiness and asceticism could not claim, much less cause, this grace; they are a totally free gift of the *liberalitas Dei* [God's bounty]. It sounded now as if secular philosophers were claiming they could sit at their desks and order up these illuminations at will without regard for their personal qualities.

No wonder this would-be phenomenological intuition put people off and led them to reject it. And from nonreligious modern philosophers who consider mystical experience nothing more than a morbid mental state devoid of any relevance for knowledge, it could expect but a scornful smile.

But whoever took "intuition" in this way could never avail himself of the living interpretation of the word behind the practice of your method. Anyone who reads your writings, not just seeing empty words but actually grasping their meaning, and especially anyone who was allowed {38} to follow your way in discussion with you, was bound to realize that you did not sit down at your desk to await mystical

Version B

those prepared for it by a high degree of holiness and austerity of life, although even the greatest holiness and asceticism could not claim, much less cause, this grace; they are a totally free gift of the *liberalitas Dei* [God's bounty]. It sounded now as if secular philosophers were claiming they could sit at their desks and order up these illuminations at will without regard for their personal qualities.

No wonder this would-be phenomenological intuition put people off and led them to reject it. And from nonreligious modern philosophers who consider mystical experience nothing more {16/330} than a morbid mental state devoid of any relevance for knowledge, it could expect but a scornful smile.

But whoever took "intuition" in this way could never avail himself of the living interpretation of the word behind the practice of Husserl's method. Anyone who reads his writings, not just seeing empty words but actually grasping their meaning, and especially anyone who was allowed to follow his way in discussion with him, was bound to realize that the phenomenologist does not sit down at his desk to await mystical

Version A	Version B
enlightenment, but that your intellect acquired its "insights" through honest effort [*erarbeiten*].	enlightenment, but that it is a question of acquiring "insights" through painstaking intellectual effort [*erarbeiten*].

[Three points of agreement]

The phenomenological method demands the keenest in-depth analysis of a given material. To begin with, we can point to roughly three areas where behind an apparent opposition complete agreement is to be found between your procedure and mine.	The phenomenological method demands the keenest in-depth analysis of a given material. To begin with, we can point to roughly three areas where behind an apparent opposition complete agreement is to be found between scholastic and phenomenological procedures.

1) *[Sensation]*

All knowledge begins with the senses. This is the basic principle that I laid down for human knowledge; it is perhaps the most quoted maxim of all scholastic philosophy.	All knowledge begins with the senses. This is the basic principle that Thomas laid down for human knowledge; it is perhaps the most quoted maxim of all scholastic philosophy.
You seem to contradict it when you stress that insight into essence needs no basis in experience. But your statement does not mean that the phenomenologist can get along without any sense material. You only wish to say that when the philosopher is analyzing, say, the nature of material things, he needs no actual experience of a material	Husserl seems to contradict it when he stresses that insight into essence needs no basis in experience. But his statement does not mean that the phenomenologist can get along without any sense material. He[5] only wishes to say that when the philosopher is analyzing, say, the nature of material things, he needs no actual experience of a material thing. And if he

Version A	Version B
thing. And if he employs an actual perception or memory of a thing that he has factually perceived, he makes no use of the thing's placement in reality accompanying its perception or memory. Moreover, he is not concerned about *this* thing that exists in fact; rather, some clear intuition [*Anschauung*] of a material thing must be present as the material he departs from. A clear intuition in the imagination might work better than a fuzzy actual perception. But any intuition of whatever kind he uses must incorporate sensible material in such wise that the above principle is in no way violated.	employs an actual perception or memory of a thing that he has factually perceived, he makes no use of the thing's placement in reality accompanying its perception or memory. Moreover, he is not mainly concerned about *this* thing that exists in fact; rather, some clear intuition [*Anschauung*] of a material thing must be present as the material he departs from. A clear intuition in the imagination might work better than a fuzzy actual perception. But any intuition of whatever kind he uses must incorporate sensible material in such wise that the above principle is in no way violated.
On the other hand I am very far from requiring any particular kind of sense intuition, such as an actual external perception, as a support for all knowledge.	On the other hand Thomas is very far from requiring any particular kind of sense intuition, such as an actual exterior perception, as a support for all knowledge.

2) [*Intellectual processing*]

All natural knowledge, I say, is acquired through the intellectual processing of sense material. Neither does your procedure go against this principle in this broad version. But may there be a conflict between our particular	All natural human knowledge, Thomas says, is acquired through the intellectual processing of sense material. Neither does Husserl's {17/331} procedure go against this principle in this broad version. But may there be a conflict between

Version A

conceptions of processing? {39}

You say that philosophical insight is not gained through induction. When the philosopher wishes to ascertain the "essence" of the material thing, to continue our example, you do not think it is his task to observe a series of material things, then compare them and lift out their common properties. He does not get to the essence, you say, through any such comparison and "abstraction."

In your view on the other hand he has no need of a plurality; a single model intuition may be enough for him to perform a quite different sort of "abstraction" from it which does in fact give him access to the essence. Your abstraction means "disregarding" what applies only "contingently" to the thing; that is, disregarding whatever could be different in it without it ceasing to be a material thing. On the positive side this abstraction means focusing on what applies to the material thing as such, on what belongs to what I like to call the *ratio* [notion] of the material thing or to its idea.

It never occurred to me to deny the possibility of a procedure like this, and I used it

Version B

their particular conceptions of processing?

In the phenomenological view, philosophical insight is not gained through induction. When the philosopher wishes to ascertain the "essence" of the material thing, to continue our example, it is not his task to observe a series of material things, then compare them and lift out their common properties. He does not get to the essence through any such comparison and "abstraction."

On the other hand he has no need of a plurality; a single model intuition may be enough for him to perform a quite different sort of "abstraction" on it which does in fact give him access to the essence. This type of abstraction means "disregarding" what applies only "contingently" to the thing; that is, disregarding whatever could be different in it without it ceasing to be a material thing. On the positive side, this abstraction means focusing on what applies to the material thing as such, on what belongs to what Thomas likes to call the *ratio* [notion] of the material thing or to its idea.

It never occurred to Aquinas to deny the possibility of a procedure like this, and

Version A

myself wherever it was imperative to uncover *rationes* in the
sense I just gave. This is the
work, in my terms, of the
intellectus dividens et componens
[the understanding dividing
and composing]. *Dividere*
means analyzing, and sorting
out essential and contingent
elements through abstraction
is such an analysis. Only, my
terms ought not to be taken in
too narrow a sense. It would
be an improper oversimplification of my methodology to
want to restrict *dividere et
comparare* to inductive and
deductive inference as we find
them in the natural sciences
and in the traditional syllogistic
forms.

Your emphasis on the *in-
tuitive* character of knowing
essences, on the other hand,
does not exclude *all* contribution of thinking whatsoever.
You do not mean simply "looking at"; you merely intend the
opposite of logical inference.
It is a question not of deducing
one proposition [*Satz*] from
another, but of penetrating
the objects and their objective
interrelations which can
become the substratum for
propositions.

When I described the
proper task of the intellect as

Version B

he used it himself wherever it
was imperative to uncover
rationes in the sense just given.
This is, in his terms, the work
of the *intellectus dividens et
componens* [the understanding
dividing and composing].
Dividere means analyzing, and
sorting out essential and contingent elements through
abstraction is such an analysis.
Only, these scholastic terms
ought not to be taken in too
narrow a sense. It would be an
improper oversimplification
of St. Thomas's methodology
to restrict *dividere et componere*
to inductive and deductive inference as we find them in the
natural sciences and in the
traditional syllogistic forms.

Husserl's emphasis on the
intuitive character of knowing
essences, on the other hand,
does not exclude *all* contribution of thinking whatsoever.
He does not mean simply
"looking at"; he merely intends the opposite of logical
inference. It is a question not
of deducing one proposition
[*Satz*] from another, but of
penetrating the objects and
their objective interrelations
which can be the substratum
for propositions.

When Thomas described
the proper task of the intellect

Version A

intus legere, = reading inside things, the words will surely be an apt expression for what you yourself mean {40} by "intuition."

Hence we should agree that *seeing* essence is not opposed to thinking, as long as we take "thinking" in the broad sense required, and that this seeing is a contribution of the *understanding,* again, taking "understanding" (*intellectus* [intellect]) in the proper sense and not for the caricature which rationalists and their opponents have made of it.

Version B

as *intus legere,* reading inside of things, the phenomenologist can accept the words as an apt paraphrase of what he himself means by "intuition."

Hence both should agree that *seeing* essence is not opposed to thinking, as long as we take {18/332} "thinking" in the broad sense required, and that this seeing is a contribution of the *understanding,* again, taking "understanding" (*intellectus* [intellect]) in the proper sense and not for the caricature which rationalists and their opponents have made of it.

3) [*Passivity of understanding*]

So I believe we can also agree on the active or passive character of intuition. Although I see the working of the *intellectus agens* [the agent or active intellect]—a genuine *action* of the understanding—in the procedure that endeavors to get to the essence from the source material, what characterizes the *intus legere,* the *insight* of the understanding that is the ultimate aim of all its movement, is a receiving.

You have especially stressed this passive element because it

So I believe we should see agreement on the third question: the active or passive character of intuition. Although Thomas sees the working of the *intellectus agens* [the agent or active intellect]—a genuine *action* of the understanding—in the analyzing procedure that endeavors to get to the essence from the source material, what characterizes the *intus legere,* the *insight* of the understanding that is the ultimate aim of all its movement, is a receiving.

Phenomenology has especially stressed this passive element

Version A

sets off your mode of inquiry, which allows itself to be led by objective *ratio,* from those trends of modern philosophy wherein thinking means "constructing" and knowledge a "creation" of the inquiring understanding. We meet again, you and I, in our opposition to any subjective arbitrariness and in the conviction that intuiting, in the sense of passively receiving, is the proper contribution of the understanding and that all of its action is but a preparation for it.

{*The following paragraph has been crossed out in the manuscript.*}
    The only question is *how far* such an insight of the understanding is possible for the human intellect *in statu viae* [in the present life]. For higher minds, i.e., for God, angels, and men who have already reached the goal of eternal life, it is the only form of actuality the understanding has. For them there is no step-by-step advance, but only an immediate insight without the possibility of deception. For human understanding, insight signifies the *ideal limit* of its performance capability. By "ideal" I do not mean that

Version B

because it sets off its mode of inquiry, which allows itself to be led by objective *ratio,* from those trends of modern philosophy wherein thinking means "constructing" and knowledge a "creation" of the inquiring understanding. Phenomenology and scholasticism meet again in their opposition to any subjective arbitrariness and in the conviction that intuiting, in the sense of passively receiving, is the most proper contribution of the understanding and that all of its action is but a preparation for it.

Version A	Version B

this limit is simply unattainable *in statu viae*. It is a "limit" in the proper sense: at this point man's mind *touches* the sphere of higher minds. In my writings I spoke frequently of an *intellectus principiorum* [understanding of principles]: for... {*The continuation is missing and the same number 58 appears on the front of the next page.*}

[*Immediacy of insight*]

{41} However, although we have initially found a sense of "intuition" we could agree on, we have yet to decide whether I could grant you what you understand by intuition and, if I could, whether I could admit it as a kind of knowledge attainable by the human intellect *in statu viae*. To gain some clarity on the matter, let us think about the problem of the *immediacy* of insight.

However, although we initially found a sense of "intuition" on which agreement could be reached, we have yet to decide whether Thomas could grant what phenomenology understands by intuition and, if he could, whether he could admit it as a kind of knowledge attainable by the human intellect *in statu viae*. To gain some clarity on the matter, let us think about the problem of the *immediacy* of insight.

[*Thomas on first principles*]

We can speak of "immediacy" in very different ways. First, it may mean that we gain insight "without further ado," in the sense that it needs no previous work, that we need not approach it step by step.

We can speak of "immediacy" in very different ways. First, it may mean that we gain insight "without further ado," in the sense that it needs no previous work, that we need not approach it step by step.

Version A

I ascribed such immediacy to the *intellectus principiorum* [understanding of principles], the insight into basic truths that I considered part of the natural equipment of the human mind. Principles are not derived from anything else; rather, everything else is derived from them and by them all derived truth is to be gauged.

When I called these principles "innate" I did not mean of course that the human being actually knows them from the beginning of his existence. I meant that he possesses this knowledge—"habitually," as I term this kind of being-on-hand—and that the moment his understanding goes into action, it performs its acts by virtue of the certainty of these truths, and it is able at any time to focus on them and intuit them actually.

This immediate insight contrasts with the mediate insight of inferred truths which, though likewise had by insight, [*einsehen*] are not known blindly when we derive them in a living thought-process from premises known by insight. Immediate knowledge has the advantage that it is

Version B

Thomas ascribed such immediacy to the *intellectus principiorum* [understanding of principles], the insight into basic truths that he considered part of the natural equipment of the human mind. Principles are not derived from anything else; rather, everything else is derived from them and by them all derived truth is to be gauged.

When Thomas calls these principles "innate" he does not mean of course that the human being actually knows them from the beginning of his existence. He means that he possesses this knowledge—"habitually" is the scholastic term for this kind of being-on-hand—and that the moment his understanding goes into action, it performs its acts by virtue of the certainty of these truths, and it is able {19/333} at any time to focus on them and intuit them actually.

This immediate insight contrasts with the mediate insight of inferred truths which, though likewise had by insight [*einsehen*], are not known blindly when we derive them in a living thought-process from premises known in insight. Immediate knowledge has the advantage that it is

Version A

free from error and cannot be lost, whereas mistakes may be made in deduction and hence error may occur.

When we say principles are known immediately, we do not mean they are the first thing in time that we know actually. This would go against our principle that all knowledge begins in the senses. Things falling under our senses are what we know first. However, although our knowledge of principles presupposes sense experience *in time,* our knowledge of them in no way gets its validity [*Recht*] from sense experience. Principles are the first truth {42} *objectively;* that is to say, they are the first of what human knowledge can naturally attain.

In the absolute sense God himself is the first Truth. First Truth of himself has provided us with the principles and the "light" of understanding, that is, the power to know granted us that we may move ahead from the principles—the "image" of the eternal Truth that we bear within ourselves.

Version B

free from error and cannot be lost, whereas mistakes may be made in deduction and hence error may occur.

Saying principles are known immediately does not mean they are the first thing in time that we know actually. This would go against the principle that all knowledge begins in the senses. Things falling under our senses are what we know first. However, although our knowledge of principles presupposes sense experience *in time,* our knowledge of them in no way gets its validity [*Recht*] from sense experience. Principles are the first truth *objectively;* that is to say, they are the first of what human knowledge can naturally attain.

In the absolute sense God himself is the first Truth. First Truth of himself has provided us with principles and the "light" of understanding, that is, the power to know granted us that we may move ahead from the principles—the "image" of the eternal Truth that we bear within ourselves.

[*Husserl on truths of essence*]

You seem to claim for what you call "truths of essence"

Husserl claims for what he calls "truths of essence," to

Version A

that immediate insight that I grant to principles. For you demand that these truths should be had directly by insight without being derived from any other truths. And you also hold that these truths cannot be nullified, at least not by experience, and then call them *a priori*. Hence we would also have to look into whether everything you call "truths of essence" really has the character of principles.

Husserl: Actually, from the traditional viewpoint only the rules of formal logic have been considered principles. But this conception is probably somewhat too narrow. Deduction involves not only principles *in accord with* which some truths should be inferred from others, but also principles *from* which they are inferred: not only logical rules but principles with content (in a specific sense) as well. Thus in the area of practical knowledge I explained the general knowledge of the good as knowledge in principle, that is, as knowledge that is our own originally and is free of error and beyond recall.

The distinction is clearest in mathematics, which besides

Version B

judge from his way of characterizing them, *that* immediate insight that Thomas grants to principles. For according to phenomenology these truths must be had directly by insight without being derived from any other truths. It also holds that these truths cannot be nullified, at least not by experience, and that is why it calls them *a priori*. Hence we would also have to look into whether everything phenomenologists call "truths of essence" really has the character of principles.

Actually, from the traditional viewpoint only the few customary rules of formal logic have been considered principles. The phenomenologist would call this conception too narrow. Deduction involves not only principles *in accord with* which some truths should be inferred from others, but also principles *from* which they are inferred: not only logical rules but principles with content (in a specific sense) as well.

The distinction is clearest in mathematics, which besides

Version A	Version B
inference rules also involves axioms from which its theorems are derived. True, there is controversy, which we cannot settle here, whether mathematical axioms are known by insight and whether they are set off by themselves before the theorems and so to speak predestined to be axioms, so that the network of inferences could not be retraced. Moreover, we would have to discuss whether and how far objects outside of mathematics admit of an axiomatic development. It has always been my view that in philosophy we are working with an open plurality of "axioms," so that it can never become an axiom-system.	inference rules also involves axioms from which its theorems are derived. True, there is controversy, which we cannot settle here, whether mathematical axioms are known by insight and whether they are set off {20/334} by themselves before the theorems and so to speak predestined to be axioms, so that the network of inferences could be arranged in no other way. Moreover, we would have to discuss whether and how far objects outside of mathematics admit of an axiomatic development. In any case, the phenomenological view is that in philosophy we are working with an open plurality of "axioms," so that it can never become an axiom-system.

[*Three claims*]

The following claims seem {43} unquestionable to me:	The following claims seem unquestionable:
1) The distinction between truths of immediate insight and derived truths arises at this point.	1) The distinction between truths of immediate insight and derived truths arises at this point.
2) Truths having a specific content number among the truths of immediate insight.	2) Truths having a specific content number among the truths of immediate insight.
3) The insight by which these principles with specific	3) The insight by which these principles with specific

Version A

content are had is *intellectual,* not sense evidence, and hence their content cannot be derived, at least not completely, from sense experience.

Thomas: The first claim I can of course readily admit. On the second I would like to say that there may well be truths of content had by insight, namely those that set apart what belongs to the truth of a thing, and you would have been thinking chiefly of these when speaking of truths of essence. However, these truths are not known by "immediate" insight in the sense just laid down; that is, they are not accessible without further ado to human knowledge *in statu viae,* but must be actively acquired [*erarbeiten*].

I have already conceded to you that this activity should not be thought of as induction, and also, implicitly, that the truths thus acquired do not owe their validity to experience so that you may call them *a priori* in this sense.

In only *one* other instance did I grant the human mind the *same* immediacy that I did to the *intellectus principiorum:* the *general* knowledge of the

Version B

content are had is *intellectual,* not sense evidence, and hence their content cannot be derived, at least not completely, from sense experience.

From St. Thomas's point of view the first claim can of course be readily admitted. On the second he should say that there may well be truths of content had by insight, namely those that set apart what belongs to the whatness of a thing, and the phenomenologist is thinking chiefly of these when speaking of truths of essence. However, these truths are not known by "immediate" insight in the sense just laid down; that is, they are not accessible without further ado to human knowledge *in statu viae,* but must be actively acquired [*erarbeiten*].

It was already conceded that this activity should not be thought of as induction, and also, implicitly, that the truths thus acquired do not owe their validity to experience so that they may be called *a priori* in this sense.

In only *one* other instance did Thomas grant the human mind the *same* immediacy that he did to *intellectus principiorum:* the *general* knowledge of the

Version A	Version B
good, as distinct from what is good and worth pursuing in a particular case. I regarded it as belonging to the natural equipment of our mind, as unable to mislead and to be lost, as an *a priori* of practical knowledge just as logical principles are an *a priori* of theoretical knowledge.	good, as distinct from what is good and worth pursuing in a particular case. He regards it as belonging to the natural equipment of our mind, as unable to mislead and to be lost, as an *a priori* of practical knowledge just as logical principles are an *a priori* of theoretical knowledge.
The fact of our own existence counted as immediately certain for me, even if it is not endowed, as are principles, with the necessity of insight. We possess it, too, "without further ado," without deriving it from other truths or acquiring it through our efforts.	Then the experience of our own existence counted as immediate for Thomas, but it is not endowed, as are principles, with the necessity of insight. We possess it, too, "without further ado," without deriving it from other truths or acquiring it through our efforts.
However, what we said of the knowledge of principles should also be said of this knowledge: it is not the first thing in time that is actually carried out. Our knowledge acts are originally directed at external objects, and only by reflecting do we gain knowledge of the acts themselves and of our own existence.	However, what we said of the knowledge of principles should also be said of this knowledge: it is not the first thing in time that is actually carried out. Our knowledge acts are originally directed at external objects, and only by reflecting do we gain knowledge of the acts themselves and of our own existence. {21/335}

[*Medium in knowledge*]

Immediacy {44} applies in another way to the experience of our own existence. Knowing immediately can mean knowing	Immediacy applies in another way to the experience of our own existence. Knowing immediately can mean knowing

Version A

without any medium. In this
sense it does not mean knowing
without any previous work of
knowledge, but knowing without any medium functioning
in the actual knowledge itself.
Three sorts of such a medium
come to mind:

1) the light of the understanding, by virtue of which
we know;
2) the forms or species, by
means of which the under-
standing knows things (not
only material things, but *res*
[things], realities generally);
3) the objects of experience
through which we know other
objects of experience; for example, reflected images and
real effects of whatever kind
leading back to their causes.

The first kind of medium
is required for any human
knowledge. But to know our
own existence we have no need
of a medium of the second
and third type. That is, I do
not know my own existence
through species, even though
in a certain sense the presence
of species is presupposed,
since, as I said, my own existence
is not the first thing that I
know and since the first human
knowledge in time, that of

Version B

without any medium. In this
sense it does not mean knowing
without any previous work of
knowledge, but knowing without any medium functioning
in the actual knowledge itself.
Three sorts of such a medium
come to mind:

1) the light of the understanding, by virtue of which
we know;
2) the forms or species, by
means of which the under-
standing knows things (not
only material things, but *res*
[things], realities generally);
3) the objects of experience
through which we know other
objects of experience; for example, reflected images and
real effects of whatever kind
leading back to their causes.

The first kind of medium
is required for any human
knowledge. But to know our
own existence we have no need
of a medium of the second
and third type. That is, I do
not know my own existence
through species, even though
in a certain sense the presence
of species is presupposed, since,
as was said, my own existence
is not the first thing that I
know and since the first human
knowledge in time, that of

Version A	Version B
external things, takes place through species.	external things, takes place through species.
Knowledge of *what* the soul is—first in the sense of the soul as such, according to its own nature—although likewise not knowledge *through* species, is knowledge *from* species. I mean, the human mind knows its own nature from the nature of the species which are functioning as it experiences external things and which themselves are made an object by the mind reflecting. This knowledge is therefore reflective and mediate.	Knowledge of *what* the soul is—first in the sense of the soul as such, according to its own nature—although likewise not knowledge *through* species, is knowledge *from* species. I mean, the human mind knows its own nature from the nature of the species which are functioning as it experiences external things and which themselves are made an object by the mind reflecting. This knowledge is therefore reflective and mediate.
The knowledge of the individual characteristics of one's own soul is also reflective and mediate, although in a somewhat different way.	The knowledge of the individual characteristics of one's own soul is also reflective and mediate, although in a somewhat different way.

[*Knowledge of the external world*]

Knowledge of the external world, as I mentioned, is mediate in the sense that it is knowledge *through* species. Here we must distinguish between sense experience, knowing a sensible thing from the outside, according to its accidents by means of a sensible species or "image" [*Bild*], and the knowledge of the understanding, which penetrates to the inside of the real thing, into	Knowledge of the external world, as I mentioned, is mediate in the sense that it is knowledge *through* species. Here we must distinguish between sense experience, knowing a sensible thing from the outside, according to its accidents by means of a sensible species or "image" [*Bild*], and the knowledge of the understanding, which penetrates to the inside of the real thing, into

Version A

its essence. The *intellectus agens* has the task of actively acquiring from sense material the form of the understanding, the *species intelligibilis* [intelligible species] that makes this *intus legere* possible.

(Were it our intention to reach {45} an understanding on the structure of the perception of physical things and of the rational knowledge of nature, we would have to discuss further the meaning of sensible and intellectual species. However, for the present we need only note the several different senses of "mediacy" and "immediacy.")

Knowledge of the essence of real things, then, is mediate in the sense that it is mediated through species. Knowledge of the species themselves, on the other hand, is not knowledge through species. But it is still mediate in the first sense, of being acquired actively. The human mind *in statu viae* does not of course possess species originally [*ursprünglich*] as do the angels.

(Immediacy in the first sense does not apply to angels or to God or to blessed spirits. For them there is no winning their knowledge step by step; to them everything is accessible "without further ado."

Version B

its essence. The *intellectus agens* has the task of actively producing from sense material the form of the understanding, the *species intelligibilis* [intelligible species] that makes this *intus legere* possible.

(Were it our intention to reach an understanding on the structure of the perception of physical things and of the rational knowledge of nature, we would have to discuss further the meaning of sensible and intellectual species. However, for the present we need only note the several different senses of "mediacy" and "immediacy.")

Knowledge of the essence of real things, then, is mediate in the sense that it is mediated through species {22/336}. Knowledge of the species themselves, on the other hand, is not knowledge through species. But it is still mediate in the first sense, of being acquired actively. The human mind *in statu viae* does not of course possess species originally [*ursprünglich*] as do the angels.

(Immediacy in the first sense does not apply to angels or to God or to blessed spirits. They need not win their knowledge step by step; to them everything is accessible "without further ado." But the

Version A	Version B
But the knowledge that angels and the blessed have from other creatures is also mediate in the second sense; that is, it is knowledge through species. Immediacy in *every* sense is proper only to the divine knowledge.) Moreover, knowledge of the species themselves is reflexive.	knowledge of the angels and the blessed is also mediate in the second sense; that is, it is knowledge by means of the light they are granted, as well as—in a certain sense—through forms. Immediacy in *every* sense is proper only to the divine knowledge.) Moreover, knowledge of the species themselves is reflexive.

[*Knowing God*]

We now turn to a third area of human knowledge, besides the inner and outer world: the knowledge of God, his existence and essence. Our knowledge of God, if we limit our discussion to natural knowledge, is not only mediate in the sense of being acquired by effort and of being known through species; it is also mediated through knowledge of other realities, of creatures. Only from his effects does the human being know naturally of God's existence. For natural human knowledge there is no *positive* knowledge of the divine *essence* at all. Only negatively, again, through the mediumship of creatures, is it possible to ascertain God's essential attributes.	We now turn to a third area of human knowledge, besides the inner and outer world: the knowledge of God, his existence and essence. Our knowledge of God, if we limit our discussion to natural knowledge, is not only mediate in the sense of being acquired by effort and of being known through species; it is also mediated through knowledge of other realities, of creatures. Only from his effects does the human being know naturally of God's existence. For natural human knowledge there is no proper [*eigentlich*] *positive* knowledge of the divine *essence* at all. Only negatively, again, through the mediumship of creatures, is it possible to ascertain God's essential attributes.

Version A	Version B

[*Knowledge of the blessed*]

Unlike both this mediated knowledge and that medium-ship of active acquisition, the positive knowledge of the divine essence granted by God himself in the *visio beatifica* is immediate. In a certain sense it is also unlike knowledge through species, for the divine essence is not known, as creatures are known, through particular species; it is itself the object and the form of the *visio beatifica*.

But it is not immediate in the same *way* that God sees himself. God *is* Light, and he imparts *of* this light to the blessed, and in his light they {46} see the Light, but in various amounts and degrees according to the measure of the light he communicates. Only God himself *is* knowledge, in which for this reason knowledge and object fully coincide.

Measured by *this* standard, of course, all human knowledge · is mediate, now in the one sense of the word, now in the other. But only in the case of the principles does human knowledge also *touch* the immediacy proper to the knowledge of the blessed: possessing it or coming to possess it without step-by-step activity.

Unlike both this mediated knowledge and that medium-ship of active acquisition, the positive knowledge of the divine essence granted by God himself in the *visio beatifica* is immediate. In a certain sense it is also unlike knowledge through species, for the divine essence is not known, as creatures are known, through particular species; it is itself the object and the form of the *visio beatifica*.

But it is not immediate in the same *way* that God sees himself. God *is* Light, and he imparts *of* this light to the blessed, and in his light they see the Light, but in various amounts and degrees according to the measure of the light he communicates. Only God himself *is* his knowledge, knowledge which for this reason fully coincides with its object.

Measured by *this* standard, of course, all human knowledge is mediate, now in the one sense of the word, now in the other. But only in the case of the principles does human knowledge also touch *that* immediacy proper to the knowledge of the blessed: possessing it or coming to possess it without step-by-step activity.

Version A

It does not apply to the great many instances of the knowledge of essence.

Knowledge of essence also falls short of the seeing of the blessed in another way: the seeing is not "face to face." The blessed know the essence of things by seeing their types [*Urbild*], the ideas, in God. There can be no doubt that the ideas they see are the ideas of real things. In our own case there is a discrepancy between the species of the things which the *intellectus agens* actively acquires and the essence of the thing as it is in itself.

For one thing, a mistake may occur in a judgment that a species is the species of *this* thing. (You avoid these judgment errors of the understanding by abstaining from applying truths of essence to reality and by limiting statements [*Aussage*] of essence to the realm of the species themselves, taking them only as "noematic," not ontological.)

For another thing, the seeing of the blessed encompasses the whole essence in one simple intuition, *uno intuitu* [in a single intuition]. In human knowledge the *intuition* of essence is separate from the

Version B

It does not apply {23/337} to the great many instances of the knowledge of essence.

Knowledge of essence also falls short of the seeing of the blessed in another way: the seeing is not "face to face." The blessed know the essence of things by seeing their types [*Urbild*], the ideas, in God. There can be no doubt that the ideas they see are the ideas of real things. In our own case there is a discrepancy between the species of the things which the *intellectus agens* acquires by abstracting them and the essence of the thing as it is in itself.

For one thing, a mistake may occur in a judgment that a species is the species of *this* thing. (Phenomenology avoids these judgment errors of the understanding by abstaining from applying truths of essence to reality and by limiting statements [*Aussage*] of essence to the realm of the species themselves, taking them only as "noematic," not ontological.)

Moreover, the seeing of the blessed encompasses the whole essence in one simple intuition, *uno intuitu* [in a single intuition]. In human knowledge the *intuition* of essence is separate from the

Version A

statement [*Aussage*] or judgment
on essence. True, intuition
of essence aims at the *whole*
essence, but this *intention* is
only partially *fulfilled*. Statements on essence set forth
separately what is contained in
the simple intuition, explicitly
throwing first one property
and then another into relief.
In this way a higher degree of
clarity is reached on the
component parts—and through
them on the whole as well—
but we have a dismembering
process instead of a simple
intuition, and the whole is
never present in a fulfilling
intuition.

Version B

statement [*Aussage*] or judgment
on essence. True, intuition
of essence aims at the *whole*
essence, but this *intention* is
only partially *fulfilled*. Statements on essence set forth
separately what is contained in
the simple intuition, explicitly
throwing first one property
and then another into relief.
In this way a higher degree of
clarity is reached on the
component parts—and through
them on the whole as well—
but we have a dismembering
process instead of a simple
intuition, and the whole is
never present in a fulfilling
intuition.

[*Immediacy of truths of essence*]

So there remain only two
senses of "immediacy" that truths
of essence are to be granted:

1) the opposite of the
mediacy present {47} in the
knowledge of realities through
their effects;
2) the intuition or insight
that contrasts with "empty"
thinking or knowing.

So there remain only two
senses of "immediacy" that
truths of essence are entitled to:

1) the opposite of the
mediacy present in the knowledge of realities through their
effects;
2) the intuition or insight
that contrasts with "empty"
thinking or knowing.

[*The course to follow*]

I have devoted a compara-
tively greater amount of the

I have treated immediacy
in comparatively greater detail

Version A

short time at my disposal to immediacy since the question is especially controverted; my comments have not put it to rest. It should be clear by now, however, that the relationship between scholastic and phenomenological methods is not an issue that can be disposed of with a few cliches. Each side should spare no effort in pursuing a "subtle" analysis of the details with a view to gaining a real appreciation of this or that point—surely the prime requisite for uncovering their mutual relationship.

Version B

than other questions since it is especially controverted; neither have my comments put it to rest. It should be clear by now, however, that the relationship between scholastic and phenomenological methods is not an issue that can be disposed of with a few cliches. Each side should spare no effort in pursuing a "subtle" analysis of the details with a view to gaining a real appreciation of this or that point—surely the prime requisite for uncovering their mutual relationship.

[*Summary*]

I only set out today to raise a few points that are important in principle and may provide some insight into the spirit of our philosophies. In summary I may say the following.

We both see the task of philosophy as gaining an understanding of the world that is as universal as possible and as firmly grounded as possible.

You seek the "absolute" starting point in the immanence of consciousness; for me it is faith.

As I said at the beginning, I only set out here to raise a few points that are important in principle and may {24/338} provide some insight into the philosophizing spirit of the medieval and the modern thinker. In summary I would like to say the following.

Both see the task of philosophy as gaining an understanding of the world that is as universal as possible and as firmly grounded as possible.

Husserl seeks the "absolute" starting point in the immanence of consciousness; for Thomas it is faith.

Version A

You wish to establish philosophy as a science of essence and show how a world, or perhaps different possible worlds, can be constructed for a consciousness thanks to its mental functions. In this context "our" world would become understandable as one such possibility. The search for the world's factual character you leave to the positive sciences, whose objective and methodological presuppositions philosophy discusses in its investigations of possibility.

My concern was not for possible worlds, but for the most perfect possible picture of this world. I was bound to incorporate investigations of essence as a foundation for this understanding, but I had also to take the facts into account that natural experience and faith disclose to us.

The unifying starting point whence all philosophical problems arise and whither they return again and again, is for you the transcendentally purified consciousness and for me God and his relation to creatures. {48}

Here we must stop for today. We shall meet again, and then from the depths we shall understand one another.

Version B

Phenomenology wishes to establish itself as a science of essence and show how a world, or perhaps different possible worlds, can be constructed for a consciousness thanks to its mental functions. In this context "our" world would become understandable as one such possibility. The search for the world's factual character phenomenology leaves to the positive sciences, whose objective and methodological presuppositions philosophy discusses in its investigations of possibility.

Thomas's concern was not for possible worlds, but for the most perfect possible picture of this world. He was bound to incorporate investigations of essence as a foundation for this understanding, but he had also to take the facts into account that natural experience and faith disclose to us.

The unifying starting point whence all philosophical problems arise and whither they return again and again, is for Husserl the transcendentally purified consciousness and for Thomas God and his relation to creatures.

Version A

{APPENDIX: *The following is presumably a discarded page from A I 9, "What is Philosophy?" (Fragment)*}

… opponents are wont to object that this principle, though indisputable, is trivial. Other assertions do not find the same *consensus omnium* [general agreement]. Their validity is not thereby determined. But surely it is some indication that we do not reach every "last analysis," which is the aim of knowledge. You yourself speak of degrees of "intention" and "fulfillment." Would you claim the final fulfillment is reached on any point whatsoever? That a greater fullness, a higher degree, cannot be imagined? If not, we would agree that we have here only an analogue of seeing truth in the highest degree, not seeing face to face itself.

This was only, as I said, a quite superficial and provisional highlighting of some points of contact between our methods. For a thorough comparison we would first have to take stock of the results on both sides and look into their particular kinds of insight.

II

Knowledge, Truth, Being

1. WHAT IS KNOWLEDGE?

[Knowledge in general]

KNOWLEDGE IS the mental [geistig] grasping [Erfassen] of an object. In the strictly literal sense it means grasping something that has not been grasped before. In an extended sense it includes an original [ursprünglich] possessing without beginning and a having-in-possession that goes back to a grasping. All knowledge is the act of a person.

Knowledge as newly grasping can in turn be taken in a broader and narrower sense. It has the broader sense when the perception [Wahrnehmung] stands for sense knowledge and the narrower sense when the object of the knowledge is said to be states of affairs or knowledge is said to appear first in judgment. In the latter case it denotes the insight [Einsicht] that something is, or that something is thus, or that something is this. States of affairs can be known on the basis of an intuitive [anschaulich] grasp of objects or on the basis of other known states of affairs. But in the end any knowledge of states of affairs harks back to an intuitive grasping of objects. Intuitive grasping can be sense perception or intellectual viewing [schauen].

[Objects of knowledge]

In all knowledge the object is given as a be-ing [Seiendes]. To the various kinds of knowledge acts there correspond different objects, different ways in which the objects are given and different ways in which the objects are. Things, their properties, processes, are objects of sense perception. Their way of being given is their appearing to the senses, and their way of being is their existing in space and time.

65

Intellectual viewing may be the grasping of persons having minds, of their acts and properties, or of objective [*objektiv*] individual structures of mind, or it may be the grasping of ideal objects. The way that individuals possessing a mind and their accidents are given {50} is the understandable expression. A person's way of being is being-there-for-itself [*Für-sich-selbst-dasein*] and being-open-for-what-is-other [*Für-anderes-geöffnet-sein*]. The way of being of objective individual structures of mind is being-there-through-persons and being-there-for-persons. The way of being of the ideal is being *in* (a concrete individual), really [*wirklich*] or possibly.

2. WHAT IS BEING?

B EING CANNOT BE DEFINED for it is presupposed by any definition since it is contained in every word and in every meaning of a word. It is grasped along with anything that is grasped and it is contained in the grasping itself. We can but state the differences of being and of be-ings.

3. KNOWLEDGE AND BEING

[*Divine and finite knowledge*]

T HE KNOWING PERSON is a be-ing. The act of knowledge is a be-ing, what is known is a be-ing. When the knowing person knows himself, the knower and what is known are the same be-ing. Only in the case of Pure Act can we say this of a knowledge act and of what is known. In any finite temporal act the knowledge act and what is known are distinct, even when the knowledge act is what is known and when it is known in a reflection, which is the awareness accompanying the act and coinciding with it in time. Hence we must say that every finite act of knowledge transcends itself.

Pure Act, which is Absolute Being and which is everything that is and outside of which there is neither being nor be-ings, cannot transcend itself. Everything that is, is in it and is known in it. Hence no be-ing can be unknowable (or more precisely, unknown). If we call {51} a be-ing "intelligible" insofar as it is known[1] and render "intelligible" as "thought [*Gedanke*]," we may then call all be-ings "thoughts." But it still does not follow from this that every be-ing must be knowable for finite minds, nor that we may speak of "thought" in the same sense in the case of God and finite minds.

A be-ing's knowability and its being known have meaning only in reference to a knowing mind that does not possess knowledge originally but must gain it step by step. It is not obvious to our insight [*einsehen*] that every be-ing must be knowable to such a mind. It is immediately obvious only that no one can make statements [*Aussage*] about a be-ing of which he knows nothing. So if I say "there may be a be-ing that I cannot know," the words are meaningful only if I know *something* about it, to be precise, enough so that it is obvious to my insight that there is a gap in this knowledge and that it cannot be filled in with my own means of knowing. For a mind able to conceive a formal notion [*Idee*] of being—the need for the notion to be materially filled in with various modes of being and the mind's inability to take stock of the possible fillings in— "being" signifies more than can enter into its knowledge. So for such a mind the equation being = being-knowable does not hold (as long as the knowledge is supposed to cover the be-ing completely). But it is not obvious to our insight that there must be some finite mind for which every be-ing would be fully knowable. Therefore only the equation being = being-known-by-God holds, but not being = being-knowable (fully).

[*Accessibility to a mind*]

This poses two questions: (1) Must some be-ing be accessible to every finite mind? (2) Under what conditions is a be-ing accessible to a finite mind?

Ad 1 [reply to the first question]. The being of persons having minds is essentially *living aware of self and directed to objects*. So there can be no mind to which no be-ing would be accessible, that is, to which nothing would be knowable. Self-awareness (in the sense of reflection) and acts directed to objects are distinct types of knowledge. But the mind itself can also be the object of an act of knowledge.

Ad 2 [reply to the second question]. First, for a be-ing to be accessible to a finite mind that knows in step by step fashion, it must have duration or at least {52} be a moment in a continuum. Second, it must remain unchanged in at least a part of its make-up [*Bestand*]. Third, the mind must be able to hold on to what it grasps. (N.B. We call the structure of objects in the temporal flow of mental life the "phenomenological" or "transcendental constitution.")

Furthermore, the mind must be able to distinguish in it what stays the same from what changes without tearing it apart. When at a later moment it will grasp something in the object that it has not grasped before, it must add what is given later to what has been given earlier. This it will be able to do only if it has already grasped in a certain way what is given later along with what was given before. Hence these phases belong to knowledge over the course of time: actual [*aktuell*] contact with the object, retention, protention, abstraction, synthesis.

[*Self-knowledge*]

When the be-ing that is known is the mental life of the knowing person, the actual contact is given at every now-moment by the actuality phase and the reflection falling together. The actuality phase is a moment in a continuum (the "act" or "living experience" [*Erlebnis*] of temporal duration and, beyond it, in the living stream of experience). The actuality phase harks back into the past and is kept in retention. At the same time what previously had been anticipated as potential [*potentional*] blends with what is now actual (by fulfilling it or countering it), and is taken up into the synthetic unity which had already been anticipated at the onset of the experience as an "ideal unit" and was continually "realizing" (= actualizing) itself. When concluded the unit remains stored in memory mode and can be re-actualized through recall. For this the "ideal unit" must be able to be abstracted from the changing time mode, but also the concrete unity must be consciously fitted into the time flow experienced. That is to say, to the possiblity of [the mind's] knowing its own acts there belongs an ontic constitution of these acts characterizing them as something enduring in time in a changing concretion or as an individuated species.

[*Timeless objects*]

We ask now about the possibility of knowing a be-ing that does not belong {53} to the living stream of experiences of the knowing subject. It could be something enduring timelessly or something bound by time. If timebound it may either remain unchanged for the duration of its being or it may be something that changes and if so may in turn change continually through a part or through the whole of its duration.

We ask first: is it possible for a mind that knows in a temporal process to know something that endures timelessly? For this an actual contact between knower and known is needed that is itself something temporal. This will only be possible if the thing enduring timelessly has a relation to the temporal; that is, either it is analogous to a *species in individuo* [a species in the individual] as we found in the units of experience, or it has an effect on something temporal. In no case can something that knows in temporal acts know anything timelessly enduring immediately in its timeless existence [*Existenz*]. The effect of the timeless on the temporal may be an effect on the knowing subject itself. (An illustration would be the possibility of knowing God on the basis of his immanence; I do not wish to go into this here.) In the case of an effect on something temporal existing independently of the knowing subject, knowledge of the temporal thing is presupposed. Likewise when the timeless belongs to the structure of the temporal.

[*Objects in time*]

This brings us to the question of the possibility of [knowing] something existing in time. We assume that the thing remains unchanged throughout the duration of the act of knowledge (we do not ask whether or not it is subject to change beyond this duration). In order that something enduring in time can be known in a temporal knowing process, an actual contact between knower and known must be possible (a *quodam modo unum fieri* [to become somehow one]). For this the knowing subject must transcend itself in and with the act of knowing. On the other hand, the object must be such that it allows a mental contact without itself being so modified by it that what it had been before the modification would no longer be able to be grasped.

[*Knowing persons*]

When what is known is of the same kind as the knower, that is, a finite person having temporal acts, then the knowing must be an analogue of the knower's own personal life; I mean, performing acts {54} with the awareness that it is a concurrent or reconstructed performing, the self [*Ich*] is "another" self, the act is "another's" act. Here the possibility of being contacted by another self is added to the conditions of the possibility of knowing one's own acts. This requires (1) an *impression* as an experienced breaking-in on the context of the living stream of one's own experiences and (2) a species that can be abstracted from the individual impression, which species is to be blended in with those to be abstracted in one's own living experiences.

[*Sense objects*]

When what is known is an object of non-personal makeup—I mean, when the thing's being is not the life of a self analogous to that of the knower—the being-contacted will have to be an impression where no species of living experience is to be abstracted. We shall call "sensation" (sense impression) such an experienced breaking-in that brings into the stream of experience something that not only does not spring from its own stream of experience but is altogether foreign to the self. We shall call "sensibility" [*Sensibilität*] (*Sinnlichkeit*) the requisite accessibility to the thing foreign to the self, and "sensibleness" [*Sinnenfälligkeit*] the requisite features in the thing known. For knowledge based on sensation to be possible, it must be possible, analogously to the knowledge of acts, to hold on to what is experienced after the actuality phase, and further to abstract a species from the individual sensation.

For an object subsisting [*bestehen*] in itself to be grasped, besides the datum foreign to the self breaking in, (1) a sense datum must be abstractable from the sensation of the being-experienced and (2) the grasping of this datum must embrace *more* than the datum itself. It must be a transcending grasping, one extending to some general form of the thing, a form that, when there is a definitely regulated advance, finds fulfillment in new sense impressions. Consequently, the knowledge of a thing as an object not analogous to the self requires: (1) a flow of sensations, (2) mental activity (a sequence of intellectual acts), (3) that the sensible be at the same time intelligible, (4) that the object have a formal structure to which the norm of the sequence of sensations and acts corresponds. When object and knowledge have such a structure it will be possible, on the basis of an actual contact (perception), to advance on a purely {55} intellectual path in the "context of experience."

4. WHAT IS TRUTH?

[*Minds, finite and infinite*]

O F TRUTH WE ARE TO SPEAK when a knowing mind has known a be-ing. In the case of the absolute and infinite Mind, wherein being, knowing and knowledge are one, being and truth are also one. (For this reason the *Logos* [Word] can say: "I am the truth.") When a temporal and finite be-ing is taken as known by the divine Mind, the truth is eternal truth preceding in time the being of what is known.

In the case of a finite mind that knows in a temporal process, the truth, that is, the possession of a be-ing in knowledge, may be called the *goal* and *result* of the knowing. If truth is taken as the possession in knowledge of all be-ing, it is the "ideal goal" of a finite mind which approaches it step by step in an infinite process but can never reach.

But we also speak of *truths* in reference to a mind that knows step by step. (Thomas even speaks of *veritas creata* [created truth].) "Truth" in this case is transferred from the being-known to the knowing be-ing.

[*The known be-ing and judgment*]

We must now carefully examine the "known be-ing," as we shall call it, in reference to a temporal process of knowledge. For something to be said to be "known," the knowledge must have come to a conclusion. Knowing, when taken as the sense perception of a thing, is never concluded in itself. It is an ongoing process demanding an "on and on." Interrupting sense perception does not conclude it. Through perception, however, something about the thing is continuously being known, and at any point it may be secured as a possession in knowledge by concluding acts.

This is what happens in *judgment*. The judgment "the rose is red" is called "a truth" but it is also said to be "true." Now, "judgment" is understood {56} in different ways, which, though objectively belonging together, are not the same thing. First the *act* of judgment. To each judgment belongs not only a simple act but a whole assemblage of acts. The thing perceived is grasped under a general idea—"rose"—but at the same time it is perceived as "this" and is placed as subject. And something is selected from the perceived stock of being, again under a general idea—"being red"— and is predicated [*aussagen*] of the thing.

These are a series of acts, analytic and synthetic, of the understanding. They presuppose a definite structure [*Struktur*] in the object: that a *quidditas* [whatness] can be separated from the *haecceitas* [thisness] and substance can be separated from accident. The rose's being-red is a state of affairs included in the rose's stock of being and can be analyzed out by means of a relevant assemblage of acts. That the state of affairs obtains [*bestehen*] is asserted by the concluding act of judgment and expressed linguistically by "is." The sentence [*Satz*] "the rose is red" is an expression of the obtaining state of affairs.

A proposition [*Satz*] is said to be true or false. Its truth means that the asserted state of affairs obtains. The proposition as assertion [*Behauptung*] and linguistic expression is a construct [*Gebilde*] formed by the knowing mind. It is true when it is in keeping with the known state of affairs in form and content. Insofar as there are a formal structure of states of affairs and connections among them, there are also forms of propositions and connections among propositions, and thus there are formal truth conditions (the object of formal logic). There is also the possibility of deriving true propositions from other true propositions in a purely formal procedure; these derived propositions are to be verified by knowledge analogous to the underlying material knowledge. Insofar as every substantial be-ing implies the entire fullness of states of affairs to be analyzed from the [content] of the fullness as well as the propositions wherein the states of affairs may be stated, we can say that propositions have an ideal or possible existence preceding [their] formation by particular finite minds.

III

Actual and Ideal Being, Species, Type and Likeness

(Fragment)

[*Real being*]

HERE WE ARE TO CONSIDER the fact that when we speak of finite individuals "actual [*aktuell*] being" does not signify the peak of being [*Seinshöhe*] of fully developed [*entfalten*] being, but *real* [*wirklich*] being, to whose duration succeeding peak-phases belong. To this rose its own color—say, bright red—is proper, its characteristic scent, etc. It is still the real rose even when its color fades and its fragrance wears off. But it was not yet real while it remained in the bud, and after its leaves have fallen off it is no more. Before it gained its characteristic color and scent, these properties, which belong to it essentially, were only in it as possibilities yet to be actualized. Both properties may reach their peak of being at the same time or at different moments. And perhaps both have already passed away by the time the rose comes to its full growth. Thus finite things are never actual (in the sense both of reality and of peak of being) in their full stock of being, but [remain] ever partially actual and partly potential.

[*Ideal being*]

"Potentiality," as it is taken in this example, denotes a lower level of being destined to pass over into the higher one—into reality and full development—*within* this individual. This potential being has the substance of the rose as the basis of its being. But there is another potentiality we should identify here. The bright red of the rose can be taken as a species: not as the property of this rose but as a particular {58} shade of red that could be actualized elsewhere as well. The possibility of being actualized in any individuals whatsoever

75

characterizes a species as such. While actualized in *one* individual, it retains the possibility of being actualized in others. And this potentiality belonging to the species [of being actualized in others] is irrelevant to the overall reality state of the individual, whereas this [*es*] does share in determining its reality state if the property in question has yet to be actualized.

In a corresponding way, the property, even with its potential being, is rooted in the substance of the thing, while the species has a being independent of this thing. The possibility of the species becoming actualized in *other* things is not grounded in *this* thing nor in the being of any other things at all, but in itself. Its potentiality as possibility to be actualized rests on its own being, which is not some lower level of the reality of things. It is the being characteristic of "ideal objects" and hence can best be called "ideal being." We should claim that this ideal being—the being of "pure" (that is, not of things) colors, pure tones, pure geometrical forms—considered in itself, is something actual. It even stands closer to pure being than does the reality of things, since it is not a flowing being, but one exempt from time and from change through time and remains at rest at the same peak.

[*Plato*]

Hence we can see why Plato viewed the world of coming to be and passing away as something less than the "world of ideas." All the same, we would hesitate to attribute actuality [*Aktualität*] to his "ideas." One of the chief objections against this platonic doctrine has always been that his ideas are something rigid and dead. However, we should take "actuality" not only as being-real and being-developed [*Entfaltetsein*] but also as being-effective [*Wirksamsein*], being-active.

This objection is closely bound up with another: how are we to understand the relationship of the ideas to things and their properties? Plato described the ideas as the types of things and would explain the being of things in terms of their "sharing" in the being of the ideas. But what "sharing" means he did not fully {59} clarify. Should the ideas be conceived not only as types or proto-*images*

[*Urbild*], but as proto-*causes* [*Ursache*], at work [*wirksam*] in the coming to be and passing away of things and in shaping them into what they are?

[*Ideal being, God, and the being of things*]

Dealing with this question would take us beyond the formal focus to which we wished to confine ourselves for the present. We note only, first, that besides the divine Being, which is Pure Act, and the being of things, wherein actuality and potentiality are characteristically present, there is a third kind of being that we called "ideal." It differs from the divine being in one way in that its being is not boundless but fixed to a definite "what." It further differs in that it is not *actus purus* [Pure Act]: it has a relation to the being of things that gives it the character of unfulfilled possibility.

On the other hand, the being of things has a relation—whose content we have yet to define—to ideal being. The relation of individual objects to the "ideas" attaches to "what" they are and what they are "like." The broadest answer to the question "what is the thing?" is "the lowest species," which is the "type" of the concrete individual (e.g., the name of a completely determined variety of rose). The answer to the question "what is it like?" is "a quality" in a species (such as a determined shade of red).

Now, what distinguishes the concrete individual from the species that it matches feature by feature? What [distinguishes] the property in the thing from the pure quality of color that it actualizes? This question is very closely connected with another: what distinguishes the being of the thing from ideal being? Is it the concrete individual's form that the lowest species enters into? And, correspondingly, is the form a property of the thing?

This is obviously no solution. The thing is not composed of a general species, which of itself allows a plurality of several actualizations plus the empty form of the individual. This form is rather proper to the individual because it is itself not anything general but individual through and through. It has a characteristic fullness and weight which the species lacks and which cannot be reduced either to an assignable content or to an empty form. It is just this fullness and weight that characterizes the being of a thing in contrast to ideal being.

[*Matter and individuation*]

Traditionally, the stuff of the thing's makeup [*Aufbau*] {60} that cannot be grasped qualitatively is called "matter." We will not examine it now in regard to what it is in its being, but will focus instead—again, only from the formal viewpoint—on what grounds the distinction of the thing from the lowest species, the distinction of the thing's being from ideal being, and on what makes it possible for a species to "occur" in a plurality of individuals.

Two further questions come up at this point. (1) Is matter in all cases the *principium individuationis* [individuation principle]? I mean, is matter what makes the thing an individual—this one and no other—or are there objects that are individuals in their "what"? (2) When we ascribe actual being (in the sense of real being) to the concrete individual, to what does it owe this being? Does it attach to the form of the individual, to the species that determines its "what," or to the matter that gives it its characteristic fullness and weight of real being?

The first question has previously (p.39) been mentioned briefly and answered to the effect that there are individuals for which matter is not the principle of individuation. The question about what they owe their being to must be asked specifically in their regard (p.63).

Material things, we must say, cannot have the being that is characteristically actual to them by virtue of the form of the individual, since only an unsubstantial and hence potential being characterizes this form inasmuch as it is empty. Matter, we said, gives the thing's being its characteristic fullness and weight; but the being of the thing cannot be due to matter either, since matter cannot exist by itself but, again, has only potential being. To come into existence, matter needs forming of two sorts: it must be formed by the species that determines the thing to its content (the *essence*-form [*Wesensform*], to be distinguished from the empty form) and by the form of the individual, into which the matter, as formed by the species, enters.

Is it, then, the species to which the thing owes its being-real? If we take the species as "pure idea," this, too, does not seem free of problems. Can something whose being is said to be "ideal" ground the thing's being? The *carrier* of a thing's being is obviously the *whole*, whose component parts we are now considering separately: the matter {61} formed into the concrete individual. We need not bother to reduce the being of this whole to anything else, if it had always subsisted [*bestehen*] as a whole, if the parts therein connected belong together indissolubly. We need not now discuss whether such indissoluble connectedness is conceivable at all, or whether the fundamental separability of its parts does not correspond instead to the composedness of a whole.

However it may be, there *are* at any rate some things that intuitively bring home to us a material thing's being formed. This we can observe with particular clarity in *artistic shapes* and *organic becoming*. When an artist forms the shape of a boy in marble, the finished work of art is the concrete individual standing before us as the result of the "forming." "This thing here" is the form of the concrete individual. The shape of the boy in its characteristic beauty is the species that makes this thing into what it is. Before it was actualized, the artist "had the idea in mind."

{*The following sheets (59–75) are lost.*}

[St. Thomas]

...Is this contradicted by St. Thomas's words: "Truth is said to be created because before having being it is nothing save in the Creator's mind, where it is not as creature but as creative essence"?[1] When we rightly understand what Thomas means by "idea" and "whatness" the passage actually confirms our view. The *whatness* is that into which a thing is formed, *what* it is, "a part of the composite whole." He also calls it a "form" (in the sense of essence-form). However, the whatness of the thing is usually not called its "idea," for the word "idea" seems to mean a form that is separated from that whose form it is. "It is that *according to which* it is {62} formed; and it is the exemplary form into whose likeness something is shaped...."[2]

Furthermore, the intention to give a particular form to the thing is proper to the relation between type or original [*Urbild*] and likeness or copy [*Abbild*]. Where there is only a chance resemblance we cannot speak of copying or imitating. In the end, the agent to which the forming is ascribed must set itself the goal of forming something according to a type, as an artist does. "So this seems to be the notion of 'idea': the idea is a form that something copies in virtue of the intention of some agent."[3] For natural things God is the "creating artist." "But since it is unfitting to suppose that God acts for a goal other than himself or receives from elsewhere the wherewithal to act, we cannot place the ideas outside God, but only in the divine mind."[4]

Consequently Thomas rejects an independently existing world of objective ideas. He admits created "forms": the essence-forms that have their being in things, and he admits ideas different from them as eternal types of things in the divine mind.

{*This is the last paragraph of the fragment.*}

IV

Sketch of a Foreword
to *Finite and Eternal Being*

(Fragment)

T HESE INQUIRIES CAN OFFER but a very modest contribution to this task. This was clear to me when I wrote them four years ago and it is still clearer today when in obedience to my superiors I take them up again to go over them once more for publication.

Edmund Husserl formed my philosophical thinking. In his school I had gained the maturity to do independent work before coming to know the thought world of St. Thomas Aquinas. While translating his *Quaestiones de Veritate*,[1] I became so absorbed by his thought world that an inner clash between it and the phenomenological way of philosophizing was inevitable. A first expression of this clash—hardly more than a study program—was a modest contribution to the *Festschrift* for Husserl's seventieth birthday.[2]

The following studies represent a second, broader and deeper, endeavor. They set out from some basic {64} Thomistic concepts without claiming to give a complete account of the Thomistic system or take a definitive stance on it. I lack the basic comprehensive knowledge of medieval philosophy essential for such an undertaking. The outward circumstances of my life have never allowed me to fill this large gap in my philosophical formation. I could make up for it only as far as my other professional duties at the time permitted. Hence all I can do now is show how far I have gotten in coping with the great questions of being with my two sets of tools: the medieval and the modern way of thinking. Perhaps it will help others to advance further.

Sister Teresia Benedicta a Cruce, O.C.D.

Carmelite Convent in Cologne-Lindental
May 20, 1935

V

Ways to Know God

The "Symbolic Theology" of Dionysius the Areopagite and Its Objective Presuppositions[1]

I. PRELIMINARY CONSIDERATIONS

1. The Dionysian Writings

[Dionysius and Western thought]

THREE MAJOR INTELLECTUAL CURRENTS were largely responsible for shaping Western thought and through its mediation continue to exert an influence today as a living heritage. These currents presuppose the revelation of Holy Scripture as their firm foundation. They represent several means whereby we grasp the very content of revelation, inwardly make it our own, and "inform" the fruits of our intellectual endeavor with the God's Word—thus achieving a living whole from the wisdom of both God and man. All three left a clear mark upon the work of St. Thomas, and perhaps along no other route have they had greater impact on later times. The three currents are: Greek thought, especially that of Aristotle, the work of St. Augustine, and the legacy of the "Areopagite."

No sooner mentioned than it is obvious that these currents are not completely unconnected. Augustine and Dionysius were formed {66} by Greek thought, each in his own way, and carried through the first great comparative analysis that would be taken up again centuries later with their help. This is just the reason why their influence differed essentially from the direct impact of the Greek philosophers.

It may sound surprising that we mention the Areopagite's influence along with that of Aristotle and Augustine, but this is hardly an exaggeration. Today, knowledge of his ideas and works seems to be limited to specialists or the occasional "fan." But his actual effect reaches further than the knowledge about him, for he dominated Western thought from the ninth to the sixteenth century, and the church recognized his authority from the sixth century and looked upon him as a leading figure in the critical debates on the purity of the faith.

In recent studies on Dionysius, we read over and over again that the big reason for his authority and influence was his name. I have been calling him "the Areopagite"—and therein lies an awkward story. A set of his writings appeared under the name "Dionysius" at the end of the fifth century (I mean, they are attested to only from this time). Their author did not call himself "the Areopagite." Several features, however, led to the belief that this Dionysius must be the Areopagite whose conversion is recounted in the Acts of the Apostles: he called St. Paul his teacher and dedicated his works to his "fellow-priest Timothy," in some passages he spoke as an eyewitness of events taken from time immemorial to be the eclipses at the crucifixion and the death of the Mother of God,[2] and he addressed all his letters to people bearing names from the time of the apostles.[3] {67}

Early doubts about the authorship gradually faded and were not heard again until the advent of humanism. For several decades now, careful studies on the intellectual background inferred from the nature of the writings themselves have convinced practically all scholars that they cannot date from apostolic times[4] and most today put them at the end of the fifth century. It has become customary ever since to refer to their author as "Pseudo-Dionysius, the Areopagite." I have used quotation marks to show that I do not take the author of the *Areopagitica* [Dionysian writings] to be Paul's disciple, and I trust I need fear no misunderstanding when I write "Dionysius" or "the Areopagite." On the identity of the person who gave himself out under this name or hid behind it, I do not wish to speculate, and as long as the author cannot be confidently identified, we will be unable to say for sure why he took the name "Areopagite."

The sobering effect of the disappointing "unmasking" of the author was to bring down wrath upon him and indignation at his "fraud." Out went the call to shed his influence as quickly and thoroughly as possible. And yet, any unbiased reader who for the first time engages the brilliant mind of this unknown thinker will at once fall under his spell. And his spiteful critics, by merely letting him speak for himself, will boost his cause, like it or not.

The reply of John Scythopolis (sixth century) is also constantly quoted against the charge of "pseudonymity": anyone attributing these works to a later writer must think him quite a desperate fellow for telling such lies about himself (there follows a list of passages wherein the author is made to appear as a contemporary of the apostles and in close association with them)—such {68} a thing would be outrageous and reprehensible in quite ordinary folk, but how much more so in someone as outstanding in character and knowledge![5] We cannot discuss here how it is possible to assign these writings to a later time without casting a stone at their author.[6]

The indisputable fact is that we possess a *corpus dionysiacum* [body of Dionysian writings]: four long treatises and ten letters (in the West alone there are 23 Greek and 32 Latin manuscripts). And we see in an unusually clear light how this corpus penetrated and affected medieval intellectual life.[7] Legend it may be that the Areopagite was the first bishop of Paris and lies buried in Saint-Denis, but it is a historical fact that it was from the abbey of Saint-Denys that these writings began their triumphant advance in the Latin West. I do not intend to pursue here the history of their impact but rather to focus on certain features of their thought world in order to bring out something of their objective significance—and indeed from a viewpoint that will interest philosophers as well as theologians.

2. The Order of Being and Knowledge in the Areopagite

[*The order of being*]

A *thread* runs through all of Dionysius's writings that have come down to us. In the prologue of his commentary [8] on Dionysius, *Albert the Great* summed it up in a quotation from Ecclesiastes: *Ad locum unde* {69} *exeunt flumina revertuntur ut iterum fluant* [the streams return to the place whence they have issued to again flow forth].[9] This flowing should be taken first as the *order of being*: every be-ing issues from God as from the First and returns to him again. *Iterum fluere* [flowing forth again] after reuniting implies not a separation but an inclining to what lies below in order to raise it up. Herein lies another basic law of the Dionysian worldview: the ranking of levels that he calls "hierarchy" and himself defines as "the whole

ordering of holy things present." [10] Its task is to lead all creation
back to the Creator.

[*The order of knowledge*]

Like the law of issue and return of which it forms part, hierarchy is not only an order of being but also an *order of knowing*. Out of
the unapproachable light veiling Primal Be-ing [*Ur-Seiendes*] from
creatures by its too dazzling brilliance, a ray that these creatures can
grasp strikes first those beings [*Wesen*] closest to him, the loftiest
pure spirits, enlightens them, and is passed on to the orders below,
widely scattered, down to the lowest creatures capable of enlightenment. In a sense this includes every be-ing. For although not
everything can receive divine enlightenment in *the way* in which it
enables some—the created spirits, angels, and human beings—to
know God and freely strive after him, nevertheless even the lowest
creatures, those lacking reason and even life, are fit to serve as *tools*
and *being-images* [*Seinsbild*] of spiritual and divine being and acting.
Hence in this sense they form part of the hierarchical ranking of
being and knowledge, and Dionysius also mentions them in his
works on the celestial and ecclesiastical hierarchies. However, only
the heavenly spirits and consecrated ministers of the Church are
the *bearers* of hierarchical acting, God's messengers, destined to
bear the heavenly light throughout creation. {70}

3. The Degrees of "Theology"

[*Mystical theology*]

We wish to focus now on one theme in the Areopagitic writings
from the background material we outlined in the introduction: *the
knowledge of God*. Dionysius is basically concerned only with *this knowledge*. He himself gave us a brief overview in his *Mystical Theology*—
an "opusculum" [short work] in length (it is only a few pages long)
but momentous in content and in the enormous influence it was
to exert. To this more than to any other work he owes his title

"father of mysticism." We should not imagine that the work is a "treatise on mysticism" or a "theory of mysticism" in the modern sense. To avoid this misunderstanding from the outset, we should clear up what the Areopagite understands by "theology." He does not take it as a science or a systematic doctrine about God; scholars stress that "theology" for him means *Holy Scripture*, "God's Word," and "theologians" means its authors, the sacred writers.

Their view is quite right; a mere glance through the Areopagite's works will show that this is usually how he uses these terms. Still, it does not seem to me to exhaust their meaning. The very name "mystical theology" suggests what it is all about, since, as we shall show, *speaking* about God is no longer meant. When Dionysius calls Daniel, Ezechiel, or even the Apostle Peter "theologians," he does not mean only nor, as I believe, even primarily that they are the authors of the books or letters bearing their names, but that they are (as we would say) *inspired:* they *speak of God* because *God has taken hold of them* or *God speaks through them.* In this sense the angels, too, are theologians, and Christ, the living Word of God, is the highest of all theologians. Indeed we shall in the end be led to call God the "Primal Theologian" [*Ur-Theologe*]. Consequently the various {71} "theologies" distinguished from "mystical theology" in the work are not "disciplines" or fields, but *different manners of speaking of God* and—expressed in them—*different ways or manners of knowing God* (or not-knowing him); *mystical theology* itself represents the *highest stage.*

Perhaps the best translation of "mystical theology" may be "secret revelation." God is known only by revealing himself, and the spirits to whom he reveals himself pass on the revelation. Knowing and witnessing go together. But the higher the knowledge, the darker and more mysterious it is, the less it can be put into words. The ascent to God is an ascent into darkness and silence.[11] When the person still stands at the foot of the mountain he can express himself in greater detail. Dionysius himself did this in his works on *positive theology.*[12] These are the treatises on the main truths of faith taught in Holy Scripture, especially the Trinity and the Incarnation (discussed, he tells us, in his "Theological Representations"),[13] on the meaning of divine names derived from the spiritual (treated in the *Divine Names*[14]), and on names transferred {72} from the things of sense to the divine (covered in the "Symbolic Theology"). This last work and the "Theological Representations" have not come down to us.

The Areopagite speaks of the mysteries of the Trinity and Incarnation in the second chapter of the *De divinis nominibus* [on the divine names][15] to distinguish the theology of *difference* from the theology of *unity*. The former treats what is proper to the *individual Person* and the latter what pertains to the *Godhead as a whole*. Related material on "symbolic theology" in the sense described is contained in chapters 2 and 15 of the *Celestial Hierarchy*[16] and in letter 9 (to Titus);[17] a detailed example is found in the *De divinis nominibus*, chapter 9 par. 5.[18]

[*Negative and positive theology*]

This approach—starting from the known world of the senses—is the lowest, and here we can go into detail. Dionysius actually says that it relaxes the mind when in the *Celestial Hierarchy* it descends from a purely spiritual view "into the expanse of many different kinds of forms" (of the angels).[19] The simpler the object—and the simpler the object the more spiritual it is—the more it can be taken in at a glance (with a *spiritual* glance, for which the mind must draw itself together more energetically than when it considers the world of sense), and the more it can be spoken of in few words. Thus the "Theological Representations" and the *Divine Names* could involve a shorter treatment than the "Symbolic Theology."

But now in the *Mystical Theology*, "when plunged into darkness beyond all understanding we will find ourselves not only short of words but utterly at a loss for words and understanding."[20] The way thereto is a *negation* procedure: we draw near to God by denying what he is {73} not. Negation is an ascent, too, in the sense that it begins with the lowest.

In positive theology the process is the reverse. In order to state something about what basically lies above all affirming, we had to begin with what is closer to him, for he is life and goodness in higher measure than he is air or stone. On the other hand, negation must begin with what is further from him: for it is true in higher degree that he is not drunk or angry than that he is unnamed and unknown. Thus negative theology climbs the scale of creatures in order to state of each stage that the Creator is not to be found there. It goes further and tests all the names that positive theology has given him and of them all it must say that their meaning does not accurately describe the One Who is above all meaning. In the end it must abolish itself, since denial no more applies to him thàn does avowal. "And when we affirm or negate something about what comes after him, we neither affirm him nor deny him; for as the perfect and unique cause of all things he is above all assertion, and he is above all denial as Supremacy simply sundered above everything and beyond all."[21]

Thus upon completing the ascent, positive and negative theologies give way to mystical theology which in utter stillness enters into union with the Ineffable. The previous theologies represent stages leading up to the summit, first of all indeed as two different ways in which we characterize the Creator when starting from creatures. Although opposed, they do not exclude each other; they complement each other at all stages. Positive theology is based on the parallelism in being between Creator and creature—on the *analogia entis* [analogy of being] as Thomas expressed it following Aristotle.[22] Negative theology rests on the fact that alongside this *similitudo* [likeness] lies a *major* {74} *dissimilitudo* [greater unlikeness], as Thomas also repeatedly stressed. They come together at the summit of "mystical theology" where God himself unveils his mysteries but at the same time imparts a feeling of their impenetrability.

II. SYMBOLIC THEOLOGY

1. The *Areopagitica* on "Symbolic Theology"

[*Puzzles*]

THE AREOPAGITE called the lowest level of positive theology "symbolic theology." As we mentioned, the work on this topic, to which he constantly refers, has not come down to us; we must attempt to get a picture of symbolic theology from what he says about it in the works we do possess.

The most detailed treatment in the extant works we find in his ninth letter, to Titus.[23] The sacred authors portrayed the mysterious

and for the uninitiated inaccessible truth in images that serve as
riddles or puzzles. Indeed even eternal Truth itself, the source of
life, shows itself thus in the divine mysteries (that is, in the Sacrament of the Altar): hidden under the veil of sensible forms. We need
a key to interpret this image-language, since if taken literally it can
be grossly misunderstood; examples are "God's bosom" whence the
Son proceeds, "the breath of his mouth," God being "angry,"
"drunk," or "asleep." Holy Scripture is full of such bold images that
may offend those who fail to understand them. But the person who
can see the beauty hidden beneath the image will find them full of
God-revealing light. Such is the very purpose of this image-language:
{75} to conceal what is holy from the profaning images of the
throng and to unveil it for those who are striving for holiness and
have freed themselves from childish thinking and have acquired
the spiritual sensitivity needed to behold simple truths.

Thus the holy teachers of both Old and New Covenant used
relevant images when bearing witness to God. The angels represented divine realities in puzzle-images, while Jesus himself spoke
in parables and instituted the most Blessed Sacrament in the image of
a supper. Moreover, gaining the light of divine knowledge in this
way tallies with our human nature. For our life is at once undivided
and divided. And the part of our soul that is free of the need for
sensible impressions had the capacity to be destined for a simple,
inner beholding of divine images, while the part subject to sense
impressions must be lifted up to the divine realities through typical
symbols.[24]

In St. Paul's words, the whole visible created world stands before
God's invisible essence [*Wesen*].[25] This is why the sacred writers
consider some matters only in the context of civil relationships and
laws but others in perfect purity; some in a human way but others
in a perfect way above the earthly. At one time they keep to laws in
the obvious sense and at another to hidden rules. We are to rise
above common views and in a manner befitting the holy seek to
delve into the meaning behind the sacred signs and images.

[Fire]

Fire is the kind of image we ought to endeavor to appreciate.
Holy Scripture sometimes uses it for God himself [26] and at other times

for his word,[27] or even for heavenly spirits—but not in quite the same
sense in all these cases. Dionysius treats and interprets the fire image
more fully not in this ninth letter but {76} in his *Celestial Hierarchy*.[28]
To describe angels, Scripture speaks of wheels and animals aflame,
of men flashing like fire, of heaps of glowing coals and of fiery
streams rushing down with violent roar. The Thrones are "fiery"
and the word "Seraphim" means "the burning ones."

This favored image is meant to express the likeness of heavenly
spirits to God. But the reason why Scripture is so fond of using it of
God himself must be that fire lends itself in many ways to illustrate
the divine essence:

> Sensible fire, if we may so speak, is in all things, passes through
> all things purely, and is taken in by all things. And although
> wholly bright it is at the same time hidden and remains unknown
> when not affecting matter in which it can disclose its power. It is
> immeasurable and invisible. It rules everything and brings every-
> thing wherein it is found to carry out its own activity. It has the
> power to change things and shares itself with everything drawing
> near to it. Through its living warmth it renews everything and
> illuminates with openly flashing bolts.... It has power to divide
> yet is unchangeable; it rises upwards, penetrates.... It is ever in
> motion, bestirring itself and other things. Power it has to take in
> other things but cannot itself be bounded. It needs nothing
> else.... It reveals its lofty being in any matter able to take it in....
> However much it communicates itself by shining it nevertheless
> remains undiminished.

In this description of fire we cannot miss an echo of the portrayal of divine Wisdom;[29] the kinds of discourse that do and do
not use images elucidate one another.

[*Food and drink*]

The *mixing bowl*, which Dionysius treats in his ninth letter, is
also taken from the sapiential books.[30] Holy Scripture says that
kindly Wisdom brings {77} a mysterious mixing bowl and offers the
sacred drink it contains. But first she sets out solid food and raising
her voice kindheartedly invites those who have need to drink.
Divine Wisdom, then, serves two types of fare: solid, lasting food

and liquid, flowing drink, and in the mixing bowl she shares her provident bounty. For the bowl, being round and uncovered, serves as a symbol of all-encompassing Providence that at once penetrates and embraces everything. As the mixing bowl remains steady and solid, so Providence goes forth to all things yet remains in herself, standing steadfast in her immovable sameness.

Now, Wisdom is said to build herself a house wherein she sets out solid food, cups, and a mixing bowl, so that it will be clear to anyone properly pondering godly things how for all things she is the perfect Originator [*Urheber*] of their being and welfare, goes forth to all, unfolds in the all, and encloses all things. However the same (Originator) is eminently in itself and in no wise in anything else. Rather, removed from everything, in itself it is the selfsame; it is, subsists, and remains in the same way and eternally, ever acting in the same manner, never going out of itself nor leaving its own abode, its immovable dwelling, its own hearth. But she (Wisdom), abiding therein (or in herself), accomplishes the entire, perfect work of Providence, at once going forth to all yet abiding in herself, at once ever standing and moved yet not standing nor moved. Rather, so to speak, does she possess, at once in nature and above nature, the effect of her Providence in abiding and her abiding in her Providence.[31]

> What then is the solid and liquid food? For goodly Wisdom is said to dispense and provide both at the same time. Solid food, I believe, stands for the spiritual, lasting perfection whereby in steady, powerful, uniform, undivided knowledge the spiritual senses of those to whom Saint Paul, drawing from Wisdom, imparts {78} truly solid food share in the divine. But liquid food, I think, refers to that far-reaching, radiating teaching that endeavors to go forth to all things and leads its pupils by the good proportioned to them through the multiple, the diverse, and the divided to a simple and unwavering knowledge of God.
>
> Spiritual and divine words are also compared to dew and water and to milk, wine, and honey as well, since like water they have the power to bring forth life, like milk to further growth, like wine to give renewed life, like honey to both purify and preserve. For divine Wisdom does bestow these things on her followers, granting them abundant and imperishable delights. And this is truly to feed;

and hence Wisdom is praised both as giving life and nourishment and as giving new life and bringing about perfection.[32]

[*Other images*]

In a similar way God's "drunkenness" is used to convey the inexpressible superabundance of all good which is in God—meaning in its cause—before he dispenses it. But the insensibility that accompanies drunkenness should be referred to God's eminence: the fact that he is beyond all senses, he is above all knowing and being known, indeed above all being.

Likewise the feast of the saints in the heavenly kingdom signifies the community of the saints enjoying divine goods with a single heart and the fullness of the goods they enjoy. Their reclining at table signifies rest from all their toil, the invulnerability of their life, their way of living in the light and in the land of the living, since Jesus gladdens them and leads them to their place, even serves them, and gives them eternal rest and the abundance of all goods.[33]

At the close of his letter Dionysius gives another brief explanation of God's "sleeping" and "waking." His sleeping signifies whatever in him lies above everything and cannot be communicated[34] with the things governed by his Providence. His awakening is, he says, the attention that God's Providence {79} pays to those in need of education and salvation.[35]

In another passage he seeks to show how "symbolic theology" expresses things by showing that even in the created realm we seek to make the invisible accessible to ourselves through the visible. We may think of the soul, he says, as a kind of bodily form and attribute parts to it, although in fact it is indivisible. Its "parts" then should be understood differently from corporeal things. The mind's knowing power might be called the head, opinion the neck (since it lies midway between the rational and the irrational), and so forth; that is, the parts of the body would be taken symbolically for the faculties of the soul. Similarly we may speak of God's breadth, length, and depth, to suggest his going forth to all things, his power ranging over everything, and his hiddenness and unknowability, which no be-ing may grasp.[36]

2. The Immediate and Mediate Meaning of Symbolic Names

We shall now attempt to bring out the meaning of "symbolic theology" on the basis of these fragments. According to the brief references in the *Mystical Theology*,[37] it involves transferring the names of sensible things to the divine.[38] We must now look into what sort of sensible things have names thus transferred, what they are transferred to, and finally how we should understand this "transferring": what relation is presupposed between what it denotes immediately and mediately, both in a purely objective way and from the viewpoint of the hearer and speaker. {80}

[*Sources of symbolic speech*]

The passage just examined itemizes a whole series of "tranferences": forms, shapes, parts, tools, places, adornments, passion, grief and anger, drunkenness and staggering, oaths, curses, sleeping and waking. Some we have already encountered in our examples. Some are the objects of external perception, things and properties of things (like the mixing bowl, the form of bread and wine, spatial extension, and fire), but others are states and processes of body and soul (sleeping and waking, being drunk, angry and the like), social acts (oaths, curses) and events (the wedding feast, and others mentioned in Biblical parables).

Thus symbolic speech derives its expressions from the areas of outer and inner experience as well as from what has been called "life experience" wherein various elements converge. Hence "sensible things" should not be taken in a strict sense. Obviously what is meant here is anything so familiar from our everyday experience that we get a mental picture of it as soon as we hear the word. These names are used in symbolic speech to denote something else that is unfamiliar to our everyday experience.

[*The divine*]

Dionysius calls "the divine" what the names of sensible things are transferred to. It, too, is a quite general term which includes many sorts of things. This is clear first from the other ways in which the Areopagite uses the word. (He applies it not only to God himself and to what belongs to God's essence and to the sacraments that he instituted—the Divine Mysteries—but he calls angels and human beings, especially the bishop, "divine,"[39] he speaks of "divine joy" at the consecration of a monk[40] and so forth. Examples can be found on almost every page of his writings. It is one of his favorite words that characterize his style.)

Secondly, it is clear {81} from his examples: Fire is an image of God himself, of his Word, and of the angels. The mixing bowl is a symbol of Divine Providence. Food and drink are images of various kinds of instruction or of the share in divine wisdom gained through them. They are also the shapes in which the God-Man himself presents himself in veiled manner. In this case the symbol is no longer spoken words but shapes visibly present; and what the shapes signify is not only a meaning that we can understand but a reality that is present. But this is already to speak of the relation between the symbol and what it points to.

Let us for now merely try to grasp where "symbolic theology" would lead us through the familiar images from the world of our experience. It is a great diversity that we might most aptly call the *Kingdom of God*. It has in God himself its reason for being and the center that unifies and governs it. God is also the true and ultimate goal which is what symbolic theology is all about. But effects go forth from God into the created world that harbor something of his essence within themselves (that is, they are "divine") and make "divine" whatever takes them in. All these "emanations" of the divine essence, all that lives like unto God in creatures and merges them with God into the oneness of the Kingdom, we can no more seize with our hands or see with our bodily eyes than we can God himself. That is why this must be made accessible to us, who are bound to the world of natural experience, through images from the world we know.

3. Symbol as Image

But how is this image-language possible? I mean, what does it presuppose objectively so that we can speak of it and understand it? To gain some clarity here we should first ask what "image" [*Bild*] means in this context. It is obvious from what we have said that neither is this word unambiguous. We had better begin {82} again with the Areopagite's own expressions. He sums up the above list of "images" in this way: ..."καὶ ὅσαι ἄλλαι τῆς συμβολικῆς εἰσι θεοτυπίας ἱερόπλαστοι μορφώσεις"[41] ("...and whatever other fashionings [*Gestaltungen*], formed [*bilden*] in holy manner, of symbolic figures [*Vorbild*] of God there may be").[42]

We take our lead from the word "symbol." The image-relationship need not be already present in its original meaning. Among the more relevant meanings that the Greek word "throwing together"[43] had taken on are: *mark of recognition* (the creed, the mark by which Christians were recognized, was called the "symbol"), *distinctive characteristic*, and *sign*. Other expressions used in this context imply that we are to think of an *image*. Three aspects are implied. The image is *formed*, that is, someone fashions or shapes it as an artist forms his work (both "τύπος" and "πλαστός" have this sense). Hence it is a *fashioning*, shaping [*Gestaltung*] (μόρφωσις), that can be clearly grasped. And it *points to God* as a *figure* [*Vorbild*] points to its *fulfillment* or as a *copy* or *likeness* [*Abbild*] points to its *original* or *type* [*Urbild*].

We should notice that the thing *formed* or *shaped* has two further aspects. First, what the "theology" comes to us in: that is, the *words* in which Holy Scripture speaks of God and divine things. Second, what the words express; that is, the *things* named (fire or mixing bowl), *events* narrated (as in the parables), or *actions* by which the prophets often graphically illustrate what they were to preach, as Christ, too, revealed {83} divine truth not only by word but also by deed, and as the church through her liturgical acts gives us matters to understand.

4. The Image-Relation and Its Presuppositions for the Person Speaking and Understanding

It would be interesting to study how we form words for the purpose of setting an *image* graphically before our eyes and doing it in such a way that it points beyond itself to what the words are meant to express *mediately* and what the images are meant to represent.

But this enterprise we must forgo now and try instead to understand the image-relation between what the words express mediately and immediately.

When Moses says "the Lord thy God is a consuming fire, a jealous God,"[44] he is in a certain sense a "theologian," a former [*Bildner*] or shaper.[45] His words conjure up the image of fire in us. The object that he "forms" [*Gebilde*] is his; it is not just any fire, since he takes it in a certain way, from one aspect, namely as "consuming." "Forming" or "shaping" here are not meant to imply any arbitrariness. We ought rather to think of Moses forming the image in this way because this was how it suggested itself to him, how it took shape "in him." It suggested itself as an *image of God*, since this was the way he experienced God. There is a likeness, something objectively common, between the inexpressible thing that happened to him and "consuming fire."

This is an *image relation* in the proper sense: something graphic, intuitive [*anschaulich*], such as may be met with in sense perception, represents something else in virtue of an objective commonness enabling us to recognize the one in the other. It is not {84} proper to the image-relation as such that what is represented cannot in principle be seen sensibly; this is rather specific to an *image of God*. It characterizes the image as such, and hence the image of God as well, that what is represented can be known from its image.

To be able to form a thing into an image of something else we must know the latter, the *type*. The theologian (taken as usual in the Areopagitic sense of one who bears witness to God) must form his images of God on the basis of his awareness [*Kenntnis*] of God. What may this presupposed awareness rest upon? Its potential sources are: *natural knowledge* [*Erkenntnis*] *of God, faith*—the *"ordinary" way of supernatural knowledge of God*—and *supernatural experience* [46]— the *"extraordinary" way of supernatural knowledge of God*.

4a) Natural Knowledge of God

[Natural theology]

As for as the Areopagite's own view, I do not think that he considers natural knowledge a possible source for his theologians.[47] However we shall briefly discuss it simply as an objective possibility.

Today we understand "natural theology" as doctrine about God
gained {85} from natural experience through our natural reason.
Its core is the arguments for the existence of God and doctrines on
God's essence and attributes inferable from our knowledge of
the created world. It proceeds by conceptual thinking, but—as in
all conceptual thinking and in all scientific procedure—it has an
intuitive basis. Intuition [*Anschauung*] here should be taken in a
very broad sense, in contrast to conceptual thinking that presupposes something given. In this wide sense it includes both sensitive
and intellectual intuition and, within sensitive intuition, what is
given as present and what is to be made present or represented.

Thinking in the natural sciences presupposes, as the intuition
initially supplying what is given, sense perception [*Wahrnehmung*]
(taken first as external perception). What it places before our eyes is
the sensible *world* and, along with it quite a bit more than actually
"falls under the senses." Perception always reaches beyond what here
and now falls under the senses and this it does in several respects.
First, what does not now but can in principle fall under the senses
and can be arrived at as perception is continued, is given to it in an
empty intuition [*leer-anschaulich*] "along with" what is actually being
sensed. But then much that can never fall under the senses is also
given along with what does fall under them, and much, too, that can
never be arrived at through any sense perception.

A first instance of what is given along with what is sensed is the
"inner" structure [*Aufbau*] and conformity to law [*Gesetzlichkeit*] of
spatial-corporeal nature as such, these mathematical natural science
seeks to understand in a conceptually exact fashion. To give just
one example. We do perceive "causality," although it can never fall
under the senses. And this view of the world, present in sense
perception itself, as "*act*ual" [*wirklich*] (in the original sense of the
word[48]) is presupposed to any search for causal laws. The natural
scientist pursues this sort of referrings [*Verweisung*] while disregarding
others. And this disregard is essential for what he understands by
"nature": something abstract compared to the fullness of the world
perceived by the senses.

This fullness has another "inner" aspect that is studied by the
exact sciences. Among the things {86} we perceive with our outer
senses are "having life" and "having soul."[49] Life and soul are "seen

along with" what we actually see in our outward perception, but they can never be seen in the proper sense from the outside. They are nevertheless truly experienced from the "inside," and what we conceive along with the outer world can in a certain way come to dovetail with what we experience inwardly.

But even besides what is specific to beings [*Wesen*] having life and soul, the fullness of the world we perceive with our senses holds more than what we can understand through the methods of natural science. This world is our "external world" wherein we are at home, wherein we live and move; it is the world we know how to "deal with." It is also "nature," the nature that we delight in and love, before which we stand enthralled and admiring, in awe and dread—nature as a meaningful whole "speaking" to us in a thousand voices, revealing itself to us as a whole and in each of its parts, yet ever remaining a mystery.

This world with all it discloses and all it conceals, it is just this world that also points beyond itself as a whole to him who "mysteriously reveals himself" through it. It is *this* world, with its referrings that lead us out beyond itself, that forms the intuitive basis for the arguments of natural theology.

[*Image and natural knowledge*]

This world is also a possible intuitive basis for image-language, for creating words and at the same time for understanding "symbolic theology." The psalmist hears God's voice in nature. Of course this is not the *only* source from which he knows God. On the contrary, he finds God in all things since he has *faith* and since God inwardly speaks to him. Still, it cannot be denied that he could have gotten many of his images just by looking at nature. "The voice of the Lord soundeth over the waters."[50] It is {87} natural for man to take the rolling thunder as a manifestation of a higher power. That is why the image of "God's voice" suggests itself and may be expected to be understood.

Symbolic speech here expresses actual or supposed *symbolic knowledge*. And in such knowledge the image does more than make present, represent, something known before but not now present, so that it may be known again, recognized, in its image. The image leads to the knowledge of what is still unknown. The "theologian" comes to know God from the image. The image in this case is not an object that *he* forms but one that God forms. God portrayed [*abbilden*] himself in the object he formed [*Gebilde*] and through it lets himself be known. That he is not already known beforehand and hence is not recognized, "known again," does not invalidate the notion of the image as a copy, likeness, made *from* something [Ab*bild*].[51] After all, in a good portrait we can not only recognize a person we know but also meet a stranger. And by looking at a good portrait we can tell that it is a *portrait* and that it is a *good* one. This is surely an objective possibility even if not everyone can do it, but only somebody with a "flair" for it, a trained eye. And what we mean by "symbol" today, it seems to me, is most properly fulfilled precisely when we take a graphic form as a symbol or "meaning-picture" [*Sinn-Bild*] and the image discloses to us for the first time a meaning that was hitherto unknown to us.

Accordingly, God is the *Primal Theologian*. His "symbolic theology" is all of creation. Theologians in the Areopagite's sense, the sacred writers, are those who have an original appreciation of this "natural revelation." To them it is given to understand God's image-language and translate it into our human language in order to lead others to God along this path of symbolic theology. We may take it that that they are "chosen vessels" by their very nature; I mean, they possess what we call a "religious flair" to an outstanding degree. In the same way especially favorable circumstances in their natural surroundings may lead them to develop this "flair" and sharpen their sight.

But we should not take this to mean that natural revelation is accessible *only* to these chosen people. The whole point of their mission rather {88} assumes that others, too, can find God along this path. We need this ability to understand *their* image-language. Their only task is to bring people who hear their words to the point where they learn to see through nature. (We should recall that after all even sense perception must be learned and is not learned equally well by everyone.)

The natural knowledge of God is but *one* possible basis for creating and understanding the images and words of symbolic theology. It is far wider than our use of a single example could suggest. We mentioned that images are borrowed not only from outer but also from inner experience. When Moses says: "the Lord is a consuming fire, a *jealous* God," he elucidates the "outer" image by the "inner." The experience of God's hand at work in one's own destiny as well as in great world events is obviously of great significance for the language of the psalms. Of course in the psalms, just as in the parables, the area of sense perception is left behind. The "image" here is an ideal one that presupposes a higher-level, spiritual penetration into what was originally given in experience.

This discussion must be reserved for a later study. In our present narrow framework we can scarcely begin to work out the characteristics and variations of all the possible ways to know God naturally and the significance of these ways for symbolic theology. For the present we must be content to note that in the natural knowledge of God we can surely see an abundantly flowing spring from which symbolic theology can draw.

4b) Faith

We can hardly determine how far the influence of natural knowledge extends and whether it is *in fact* ever effective all by itself. In any case all "theologians" stand on the ground of *faith*. For the sacred writers of the Old Testament, God is primarily the God of Abraham, Isaac, and Jacob, the God of their fathers, of whose feats they have heard {89} tell from their youth and in whose service they have been brought up.

We are not taking "faith" here broadly as "belief"[52] but in the narrow sense of *fides*, of accepting and retaining *supernatural revelation*. By "supernatural revelation" we mean God's communication of himself through the *Word* in the proper sense, above all the communication of God's mysteries hidden in himself that are inaccessible to natural knowledge by itself. (We may disregard naturally knowable [truths] that are in fact contained in revelation.) *God's word* is a *revealing* of supernatural truth and at the same time an *addressing* that requires faith as the acceptance and retention of the revealed truth. Insofar as faith confers the possession of truth, it merits the name "knowledge," but it is *dark* knowledge insofar as the conviction that it brings is not founded upon insight into the truth accepted on faith.

When speaking of God's "Word" and God's "addressing" we do not mean that in all supernatural revelation God speaks positively and immediately in a *human way*. God's Word and speech is also the word of his emissaries, his prophets and apostles, spoken in his name to those called to faith, and thus primarily means Holy Scripture. Now when we call the sacred authors themselves "faithful," here, we mean that they led a life of faith before their extraordinary calling and after their calling they did not stop living from their faith. The higher light they received does not shine constantly; it raises them suddenly and momentarily above their ordinary state, although it does leave lasting after-effects.

Our only point here is that faith by itself, apart from any extraordinary illuminations, can be a source for the image-language of symbolic theology. As the psalmist was reflecting on the fortunes of the Chosen People familiar to him from sacred history—God's wondrous promises and acts of gracious guidance, the people's repeated apostasy {90} followed by terrible judgments—certain images of God could spontaneously suggest themselves: he is a "father of orphans"[53] and a faithful, caring shepherd[54] as well as an angry judge delivering his own "as sheep for slaughter" and rising up against them in burning wrath.[55] And in turn the people, who of course belonged to the same tradition as the holy singer himself, as they heard and sung the psalms, were able to understand his language because of their faith. He put into words what was alive in their hearts or awoke what was there asleep.

4c) Supernatural Experience of God

4c1) Revelation, Inspiration, and Supernatural Experience of God

[*Inspiration*]

But faith, accepting God's proclaimed Word, goes back in the end to something else. If God speaks *through* his emissaries, their word, to be accepted as *his* Word, must somehow stand out from ordinary human words and the emissaries themselves [must be] identifiable as God's messengers. For folks of simple faith it is warrant enough that something is found in Scripture and forms part of their faith, that Scripture is God's Word and its authors are "inspired" or guided by the Holy Spirit. It is not up to them to verify this inspiration or ask how this or that word "got into the Bible." Still, it must be possible to answer both questions.

The second question, proper to Biblical criticism, we need not go into here. We may take it for granted that certain words form a genuine part of Scripture. Then they count as inspired and as revealed not only for the simple faithful but also for the theologian (that is, a theologian with faith)—taking "theologian" in the modern, not Dionysian, sense. "As revealed" means that God wishes to communicate something to us through these words. "As (91) inspired" means that God moved the author to write them down and perhaps moved a person to speak the words he imparted to him.

Must the inspired person who is the instrument of a divine revelation be aware of the fact? Must he know that he has been illuminated, must he himself have received a revelation? We may well imagine cases where none of this is true. It is not impossible that someone utter a revelation without realizing it, without having received a revelation from God, without even being aware that he is speaking in God's name or feeling supported by God's Spirit in what he says and how he says it. He may think that he is only voicing his own insight and in words of his own choosing.

Thus Caiphas says in the Sanhedrin: "You know nothing and do not consider that it is better for you that one man die for the people and not the whole people perish."[56] And John adds: "but this he said not of himself but being high priest that year he prophesied that Jesus would die for the people.... " Hence Caiphas spoke in God's name and followed divine instructions without either knowing it or wishing to do so. John, however, knows that Caiphas was speaking God's word and perhaps also that he was himself enlightened by God as he wrote this. Does John know of the prophetic meaning of Caiphas's words through a revelation accorded him? Quite possibly. But it may also be that the fulfillment of those words in the death of Jesus and John's view of the overall work of salvation made him realize their prophetic character.

It is surely not the normal case when someone is an instrument of divine revelation without knowing or willing it. For us it stands in contrast with the grand vision of Isaiah.[57] The prophet beholds the Lord on the throne of glory, speaks with him face to face and receives the words that he is to pass on to his people. {92} Seeing and hearing should, it would seem, be taken here in the literal sense. We should not take what the prophet is describing as a symbolic representation of what he has seen in a purely intellectual way.

So here too God is the "symbolic theologian" who makes himself, the incomprehensible One, known in a visible image and in human words. He reveals himself to the man standing before him and gives him a mission. Isaiah receives the revelation and his mission consciously. And when he steps before the people he knows that what he preaches is "God's word" in the strict sense. Revelation and inspiration as well as the awareness of both are here combined.

[*Experience*]

Our question now is: what makes the prophet certain that he is standing before God? Seeing with the eyes or in the imagination does not necessarily have anything to do with this. When both are absent there may still be an inner certainty that it is God who is speaking. This certainty can rest on the "feeling" that God is present; one feels touched in his innermost being by him, by the One present. We call this the *experience* [*Erfahrung*] of God in the most proper sense. It is the core of all mystical living experience [*Erlebnis*]: the person-to-person encounter with God. A sensible vision, like that of Isaiah, may accompany it as a extraordinary attendant phenomenon.

On the other hand is a vision like this conceivable without a personal inner experience of God? It is not impossible that the prophet see the Lord before him or hear his words without being inwardly touched by him in mystical fashion. This is obviously the case with the boy Samuel, who hears God calling him without realizing that it is *God* calling. Hence he does not recognize God. In Isaiah's case we might say that the miraculous character of his apparition and the accord between what he sees and hears and what he knows about God from faith could convince him, without being inwardly touched, that it is God himself.

Although we should not dismiss this interpretation as impossible, it does seem to be a somewhat artificial construction. When we read that young Samuel did not yet know the Lord,[58] it seems to me to suggest {93}that Eli did know him and that Samuel was going to meet him. *After* Samuel received the revelation, we get the definite impression that he does know the Lord now—not from deductions and rational considerations but from a personal encounter, by being seized in his innermost being, from an encounter that stirred the child to become a prophet.[59] In such a genuine living experience of receiving a mission, inspiration, revelation, and the consciousness of both are combined with a true experience of God. Many intermediate stages are possible between this fullness and the other extreme of receiving a revelation without knowing or willing it.

To begin anew from below. A person may be inspired and know he is inspired without receiving a revelation. The sacred writer knows that he is moved by God's Spirit to say or write something; *how* he expressed it may also be inspired and experienced as such. But *what* he has to communicate is not revelation for him. It may be events that he knows from experience or moral truths that he intuits with his natural understanding. (The historical and sapiential books of the Bible must in part have arisen in this way.)

The reverse—revelation without inspiration—we should say is impossible. Wherever God unveils himself or a hidden truth, he does so through his Spirit; and whenever a human being is chosen to convey such a truth to others he must be guided by the Spirit. Divine truth may enlighten him as a purely intellectual truth, without him hearing any words or seeing any objects. And the words in which he casts his message may be left up to him. Whenever he hears a revelation in words or is shown an image, all he may have to do is to pass on the image or the word without understanding them himself. But the intellectual meaning can also be disclosed to him by inner enlightenment or by words added to explain it. {94}

4c2) Personal and Mediate Experience of God

There is something more than the natural knowledge of God in all these cases and something beyond faith as well, but there still may not always be a personal experiential knowledge of God. We should first question whether in all these cases we should speak of knowledge of God at all. We might say that any experience like this will always be taken as coming from God. When a divine truth appears cast in "supernatural light," I mean, clearly distinct from natural knowledge and breaking into its context, the light will be taken as "divine light."

When words are spoken or a figure is seen and the one speaking or appearing does not claim to be God himself but an angel or saint, he nonetheless comes as a messenger of God. The person receiving the revelation knows that he is undergoing divine action through the messenger—or also through an "intellectual vision." (This applies to inspiration as well, so long as it is not experienced as of possible demonic origin.) Still, the affected person does not stand before the Lord; God remains the hidden God.

On the other hand Isaiah looked upon God himself and heard his word; and if our reading of his account is correct, he became certain in his innermost being that God himself was present. And only when this happens may we speak of a personal experiential knowledge of God.

We called this "feeling of God's presence" the core of all mystical experience. However, it is only the beginning of the mystical life of prayer, the lowest stage. There are various degrees and transitions between this feeling and the summit of "infused contemplation," the lasting union with God. Each higher stage represents a richer, deeper self-revelation and self-commitment of God to the soul, and for the soul it means an ever deeper and fuller penetration into God and acquaintance with him, which demands from the soul an ever more total surrender.

Unlike revelations wherein God does not disclose himself but only unveils a single truth or a single event inaccessible to natural knowledge, personal experiential knowledge is marked by an immediacy, in the {95} sense that what is present itself is said to be experienced immediately, not what is merely grasped through its effects or made present by messengers. But God is not "immediately intuited" in the same way as something falling under the senses or even as something the mind knows by insight.

We call the personal encounter with the Lord the "experience of God" in the most proper sense. However, the kinds of mediate knowledge we mentioned should also be counted as supernatural *experience* and thereby distinct from faith. All forms of supernatural experience—but especially personal acquaintance—stand to faith as in the natural order our very own experience stands to knowledge based only upon what we are told: as the *fulfillment* of what we now grasp only in thought without ourselves becoming originally [*ursprünglich*] aware of it.

Personal encounter as fulfillment also contrasts with mediate experiential knowledge in the sense that what is itself known as present gives fulfillment to what is only mediately known or made present. Moreover, personal encounter accords no final fulfillment, but merely points beyond itself to a truer fulfillment in higher mystical experience and eventually in the *visio beatifica* [beatific vision]. (We shall not discuss here whether some unfulfillment remains in the beatific vision since it is not seeing God as he sees himself.)

4c3) Supernatural Experience of God; Natural Knowledge of God

Faith, unlike the *natural experience of God,* in a certain sense is already marked by fulfillment, though not, of course, as our own experience fulfills what we merely know, but rather as what we *clearly understand* compared to what we only have vague "hunch" about (not yet taking "natural knowledge of God" here for natural theology but for the "grasping along with" of a higher power in plain natural experience). Again, faith is marked by fulfillment as an *enrichment of the content* of knowledge (insofar as it tells us something new about God over and above our natural experience and natural theology). And lastly faith is fulfillment as a *confirmation* by {96} a higher authority of what we have already known.

On the other hand we should compare the transition from knowing God naturally to experiencing him supernaturally to meeting a human being personally whose existence we previously only sensed in certain effects or perhaps gathered from these effects. Faith can serve as a bridge for this transition. Now, if we think of a transition from natural knowledge of God to a supernatural experience of God that is not mediated by faith, as when grace is bestowed on someone who lacked faith, and if this experience is "accepted," then the several kinds of fulfillment are therein combined, and the whole event will be much more strongly marked by inner disruption and transformation.

All kinds of knowledge of God are interconnected by the intentions through which they point beyond themselves and in the last analysis—as long as we remain in earthly knowledge—are ordained to the experience of God.[60] This does not mean that natural knowledge of God and faith must precede supernatural experience nor that they have their objective warrant therein. It means rather that there lies in them according to their own essence an aiming at the experience of God as well as the possibility of their being found again transformed in that new way of knowledge.

4c4) Significance of Supernatural Experience for Symbolic Theology

[*Experience and image*]

We should settle what we mean by the supernatural experience of God in order to determine how it can contribute to "symbolic theology" (taken as usual in the Areopagitic sense of image-language about God). Inspiration, "impersonal" revelations and visions, in comparison to the natural knowledge of God and to faith, can open up new images and at the same time lend certainty that they are "apt." What the prophet hears and sees is as it were the great school of symbolic theology where images and words become available to the sacred writer so that he may say the unsayable and make the invisible visible.

But it is still more important to be touched by God inwardly without word and image. For in this {97} personal encounter the person comes to know God intimately, and this knowledge enables him for the first time to "shape the image according to the original [*Original*]." On this basis, images and words can suggest themselves that are suitable for representing God in the way that the person has come to know him. This intimate awareness [*Kenntnis*] also gives the theologian a standard for judging or the right "feel," as he seeks appropriate images and words in consciously forming his portrayal.

[*Faith*]

When we again ask what sort of *understanding* image-language drawn from these ultimate sources presupposes, we see that the person who already possesses an experiential knowledge of God will have the *most proper* understanding. He alone can recognize *his* God, the God whom he knows personally, in the "portraits." However, a certain understanding is also quite possible on the basis of faith and even of the natural knowledge of God. The person who knows and loves God from and in his living faith will be eager to come to know him from ever changing perspectives and in new "features," and again and again he will turn to the Holy Scriptures that makes this possible.

In a way, recognizing, knowing again, takes place here, too. The person of faith of course already has an "image of God" and this he blends with the new images wherein he finds God portrayed. This is precisely how he can enrich *his own* "image" with new features from these images. (I am using "image" in a different sense in these phrases. When I say "my image of God," I do not imply any duality of image and what it represents; it signifies God as I know him and think of him.) Such blending does not leave the ground of faith behind; it is an advance within faith, clearly distinct from grasping the meaning of words through a purely natural understanding, but it is also distinct from knowing God experientially.

When a person lacking faith reads Holy Scripture—for example for the purposes of philology or religious studies—he does not come to know *God*. He only learns how God is conceived in the Bible and by those who accept the Bible in faith,[61] unless faith is awakened in him by what {98} he reads, but in this case there is a transition from one outlook to another.

Even within faith there are various ways of understanding and coming to know. The person reading Holy Scripture with faith accepts whatever he reads "in faith," that is, as revealed truth. But this on no account means that he grasps everything in a *living* way affecting his *soul* [*lebendig-seelisch*]. His reading may be largely an empty grasp of the meaning of the words, without any effect on his life experience.[62] We feel the difference clearly when all of a sudden we see a passage we have often read "in a new light"—in a light that shows us something about God that was hidden from us before or {...}[63] in our own soul. We can also be affected in a quite personal way by a divine demand that we did not realize before. Or a new relationship among truths of faith may strike us that until now were unconnected.

All this is possible "in the light of faith." Our knowledge of God is enriched by it, our relationship with God deepened and better ordered; yet with faith we still do not stand before God himself. But this, too, may happen: a word of Scripture may so touch me in my innermost being that in this word I feel God himself speaking to me and sense his presence. The book and the sacred writer, or the preacher that I was just hearing, have vanished—*God himself is speaking*, and he is speaking to *me*. At the time, the ground of faith is not exactly left behind, but for the moment I am raised above it to the experiential knowledge of God.

This is at bottom the goal of all theology: to clear the way to God himself. The Areopagite also explicitly called it the goal of his "symbolic theology." Theology addresses a select group, and for its adherents—that is, for those who have already experienced a certain enlightenment and hence are striving for holiness—it would do more than instruct them in the content of faith. By unveiling a suprasensible world for them through its images, it would teach them to free {99} themselves more and more from the sensible world and in the end it will bring them to the point where they no longer need sensible images at all. It will "lead them by the hand"[64] first from the sensible to the spiritual and suprasensible and finally to the highest summit, to oneness with the One. This last stage of course lies not within the power of symbolic theology, but is God's affair; theology can but lead in the right direction.

Now, when we called experiential knowledge a "fulfillment" of faith, the term included the notion that faith aims at the same thing that comes as given in experiential knowledge. This is a general feature of the relation of "intention" and "fulfillment." When I see something with my own eyes that I only heard about before, for example a famous work of art or a beautiful city, the reality I now have before me already formed part of my mental world. It had already gotten to me in a certain way by what I was told or read, and I was inwardly stirred by it.

And this is all the more true of faith. Holy Scripture counts as "God's Word" for us because therein he draws near to us, makes himself known to us, makes his demands upon us. Of course the word is spoken "in his name" only so long as I take it purely on faith. God is not sensibly present nor does he speak in his own Person. And yet I do come into contact with him through this transmitted word and by it I am inwardly moved. And this property of faith of going beyond itself—St. Thomas calls faith "the beginning of eternal life in us"[65]—is just what brings us to "know God again," recognize him, when he suddenly makes his presence felt or even when he shows himself visibly, and it is what enables us to understand, even without any experiential knowledge of our own, what others speak of from their experience of God. {100}

What we have said here of faith may apply in a certain way to the natural knowledge of God. A person who has grown up without religious instruction but is sensitive to the traces of God in nature, in his own heart, and in human life may perceive his failings as "sins" and a loss he suffers as "God's punishment." He can appreciate it when God is said to flare up in anger and to be a consuming fire. However imperfect and vague his natural knowledge of God may be, however much it needs to be corrected and enriched, clarified and explained by faith, it already embodies an aiming at what in the experiential knowledge of God will become reality. Also, in the natural knowledge of God a certain encounter with God takes place that enables him to "know him again, recognize him," should God ever stand before him.

5. Symbolic Theology as Concealing Veil

[*Religious sense*]

Given that a large number of people can in principle understand the image-language of symbolic theology, does it make any sense to say that it "conceals what is holy from the profaning eyes[66] of the throng"?[67]Are there still people who cannot understand it? No doubt there are—for Holy Scripture is no safer today than in the Areopagite's time from the gross misinterpretation of its images that he spoke of. And even without false interpretations there may be total lack of understanding. There are a number of reasons for this.

We mentioned that "our world" leads beyond itself in many different ways through "referrings." But these referrings are not so totally obvious and unambiguous that they never fail to lead people to the goal. As we said, having a natural {101} predisposition and being taught by those around us are as important here as in other areas. A person with no "practical sense" does not see "what things are good for" or how he should deal with them. If he is not well "trained" he will always remain at a loss, helpless in the outside world. Similarly a person may be lacking in "religious sense" and unless it is offset by a good upbringing, he may well remain blind to the referrings that lead out of the world to God.[68]

For such a person then—without a special help of grace—Holy Scripture, too, is a book sealed with seven seals. He halts at the immediate sense of the words and cannot see through the images. He does not know how to allow for the *major dissimilitudo* [greater unlikeness], and the idea he forms will be unworthy of God, or, if his idea puts him off, he will even, for this very reason, become an atheist. Another possibility is that he will reject not God himself but the testimony of Scripture.

[*Responsibility*]

Although we ought not to think it impossible that an unbeliever (meaning someone completely ignorant of God) could lack personal guilt and thereby be impervious to the image-language of Holy Scripture, we should not reject *all* human guilt. If we disregard original sin here and the clouding of the mind that it causes, no human being grows up completely cut off from others, and "society" is at fault for failing to furnish the testimony that could have opened his eyes.

In most cases however the "unbeliever" himself will share the responsibility for his blindness. A person after all {102} can hardly live in such a way that no testimonies about God at all would reach him. He is at fault if he shuts his mind to them or at any rate does not take the trouble to look into them. And if subsequently "blindness" sets in, that is, instead of merely not-knowing, he becomes unable to know, then this, too, is his own doing. This of course is truer still when the person not just happens to lack faith, but rejects God on principle or shows hostility toward God.

We need not ask here how something like this is possible. We are trying to understand how "symbolic theology" can conceal God instead of revealing him. Obviously the "innocent unbeliever" is in fact unable to see through the veil. However he is not of those who *should* not see. The word "theology" rather seems to imply that we are taught to see. In the case of someone who from mental lethargy and apathy or carelessness fails to gain any knowledge of God, his inability should rather be taken as punishment. But being struck blind we should understand especially of malicious persons who *will* not to believe and who read Holy Scripture in order to use it as a weapon against revealed truth.[69]

[*Seeking God*]

We were attempting to show that in all genuine knowledge of God it is God himself who draws near the knower, although his presence may not always be felt as it is in experiential knowledge. In natural knowledge he draws near in images, works, and manifold effects; in faith by making himself known personally {103} through the Word.

But in the case of any knowledge of persons, rather than disclosing [*erschliessen*] oneself, one may *close* oneself [*verschliessen*] — even withdraw behind one's own work. In this case the work still means something, retains an objective significance, but it no longer opens up access to the person, it no longer provides the contact of one mind with the other.

God wishes to let himself be found by those who seek him. Hence he wishes first to be sought. So we can see why natural revelation is not absolutely clear and unambiguous, but is rather an incentive to seek. Supernatural revelation answers the questions raised by natural revelation. Faith is already a finding and corresponds to God letting-himself-be-found, not only in the sense that he has something said about himself through his word but that through his word he himself has himself found.

Faith is a gift that must be accepted. In faith divine and human freedom meet. But it is a gift that bids us ask for more. As dark and lacking the evidence of insight [*uneinsichtig*], faith awakens a yearning for unveiled clarity; as mediated encounter it awakens a longing for an immediate encounter with God. Indeed the very content of faith awakens desire by promising the beatific vision.

On the other hand we can now see why God withdraws from those who fail to do his bidding to seek him, who remain apathetic in the face of the testimonies he gave of himself or who seek in them not God but means to their own ends, indeed even against God. God's word becomes a dead letter for the person who does not accept it as *God's* word. It no longer points beyond itself in a living way to the realm wherefrom it issues: the kingdom of the Divine Spirit. In many of its images, pagans may find confirmation of their idolatrous belief; dialecticians spot contradictions in different passages; moralists and educators disapprove of much it contains, since the hidden meaning is lost on them. {104}

6. Degrees of Veiledness and Unveiling

[*Hiddenness and symbolic knowledge*]

The "hidden sense" may be more or less deeply hidden. We have pointed out that "symbol" has very different meanings for the Areopagite. The word may denote visible images of the Invisible (like "consuming fire"), which however bear a genuine image-relation to the Invisible. And it may denote images (such as the mixing bowl referred to Divine Providence) wherein the relation cannot be immediately intuited but is produced by a reasoned comparison and must be found by reflection. Today in these latter cases we would speak of allegory rather than symbol.

Dionysius also gave examples of symbols that are no longer sensible at all. Parables are like this. Jesus himself gave the key to his parable of the sower at his disciples' request.[70] The warning with which he closed his story, "he who has ears to hear let him hear," already made it clear that the real point did not lie on the surface nor was it given to everyone to see it. When hearing the parable, we must first grasp the literal sense of the story exactly. This already calls for intense synthesizing activity. But we must also realize that the whole thought structure points beyond itself in a certain direction. We must disengage a "type" [*Typus*] from the story—in the sense of a general form—that is to serve as a guide for building a second structure behind the first which will reappear in the same form but with another meaning, the one the storyteller intended.

Not many are up to identifying and reproducing types in this way when humans speak in parables—far fewer, even with the best of intentions, can do it when God is speaking! Not even the disciples could do it, even though to them "it was given to {105} know the secrets of the kingdom of heaven."[71] Our Lord had to let them in on the hidden sense. In a similar way he later taught the disciples on their way to Emmaus to understand the messianic prophesies and their bearing on his passion and glorification.[72] After the descent of the Holy Ghost the Apostles could work out these explanations for themselves.

We mention briefly the diversity of symbolic relations here only to show that there are different kinds and degrees of hiddenness corresponding to the various kinds and degrees of symbolic knowledge. The most general approach is opened up in the image-relation proper. The parables present the divine truth in a locked box, as it were. Often it is left up to us to look for the key. Sometimes the key is given in an added explanation or in an inner enlightenment. Moreover, an "office of the keys," the gift and task of interpreting the Scriptures, may be vested in individuals or states of individuals.

[Hierarchies]

From this perspective we can appreciate the meaning of the Areopagite's "hierarchies." God reveals himself first of all to the pure spirits, whose natural understanding is more powerful than our own and in whom the divine light finds no inner resistance. They are given the office to pass on the light they receive. Their office in turn is continued in the "church hierarchy"—in the ranks of persons called to an angel-like life and service.[73] They are to receive {106} and administer the divine mysteries with a purified spirit. This also entails proclaiming and interpreting the divine word. And as there are different kinds and degrees of veiledness, there are different kinds and degrees of unveiling, various ranks of offices, grades of exclusion and admission.

FINAL REMARK:
SYMBOLIC THEOLOGY AND OTHER THEOLOGIES

The diversity of symbols presupposes a ranking within "symbolic theology." The gradation reappears in the other "theologies" that the Areopagite distinguishes from symbolic theology. The "spiritual names of God" (Goodness, Being, One, etc.) are not readily accessible even in their immediate sense. Thus they are intended for a select circle. A closer study is needed to bring out how they are related to God and how God is known through them. We might be able to show that although we have no mere sign-relation or likeness-relation here, there is still a "secret revelation."[74]

This is why "positive" theology also needs to be complemented and corrected by a "negative" theology. And something will appear in both theologies that turns any knowledge of God into the experience[75] of God: the personal encounter with him. When this at last becomes the person's own living experience and is no longer mediated by images and parables nor even by ideas—nor by anything that may be given a name—then and only then do we have "secret revelation" in the most proper sense, "mystical theology," God's self-revelation in stillness. This is the summit whither the degrees of the knowledge of God lead. {107}

So again we can say: God is the *Primal Theologian*. All speaking *of* God presupposes God speaking. God's speaking in its most proper sense is that before which human speech must grow dumb; it finds no place in the words of man, nor in the language of images.

God's speaking seizes the person whom it addresses, and demands personal surrender as a condition for hearing him. But this seizing is usually associated with the calling of a "theologian." Through those to whom he speaks on the mountaintop God wishes to speak to the people they left below. That is why he deigns to speak to them, through them, and even without their mediation, in human words and in images men can understand. God gives his theologians the words and images that enable them to speak of him to others. And to these others he speaks as a "symbolic theologian"— through nature, through their inner experience and through His traces in human life and world history—thereby enabling them to understand the language of the theologians.

NOTE

Our presentation in these pages is but a first approach to the problems that arise when we attempt to work with a minimum of theological presuppositions. Now, if we wished to follow up the notion of "God—the Primal Theologian" *theologically*, we would have to lay our foundation on God's speaking in its most proper sense: the speaking of the Divine Word. And as its primal symbol we would have to take the Word made flesh.

{108}   {Appendix: Fragment (Manuscript II)}

[*Positive and negative theology*]

{ ...to characterize the Creator from the creature's standpoint— when we consider only the lower degrees and disregard the highest, where, positively, God unveils his own mysteries, and, negatively, he makes the impenetrability of the mystery felt. In this sense both ways complement each other at all stages. Although opposed, they do not exclude each other. Positive theology is based on a commonness of being between creator and creature—the *analogia entis* [analogy of being], as Thomas expressed it following Aristotle. Negative theology rests on the fact that alongside this *similitudo* [likeness] there is a *major dissimilitudo* [greater unlikeness], as Thomas also repeatedly stressed.[76]}*

[*Dionysius on the natural knowledge of God*]

A person coming from Thomistic tradition will naturally ask whether "such lower-stage knowledge of God is possible as purely *natural.*" Thomas, and with him the church's highest teaching office, have given a decided yes to the question. In one passage Dionysius seems to allow this possibility. In letter [9] (to Titus) he distinguishes a *secret, veiled theology* from a public, *easily understood theology*. The former is *symbolic* and *forms unto perfection*; Corderius says that it refers to the mysteries.[77] The latter *proceeds by philosophical demonstration*. The one convinces of the truth of what is said, the other acts and confirms by its unteachable guidings in God.

On the other hand, in the introductory chapter to the *Mystical Theology* (as in many other places) Dionysius warns Timothy to keep his teaching secret from the uninitiated; that is, from those who believe "that with their natural knowledge they know him who has made the darkness his hiding place"—all the more so from those who "describe the highest cause of all things in terms derived from the lowest of be-ings and claim that it in no way surpasses their own

---

* {This passage was crossed out by Edith Stein.—Ed.}

godless, multiform constructions."[78] We must of course bear in mind {109} those whom the Areopagite has in mind when he says this. In the first group we should see Gnostics, who claimed they could penetrate the highest mysteries, and in the second, pagans who made the world of sense their idol. But his attitude on the other hand need not amount to a rejection of a natural knowledge of God that is aware of its own limits.

Might we also make a similar comment on the opening words of the *On the Divine Names?* Dionysius stresses here that he is taking the Word of God as a "guideline" and wishes to prove that what it says about God is true *"not with the persuasive words of human wisdom"*[79] but *"in the proof of the power* that the Spirit has breathed into theologians and which, in ways that cannot by spoken or known, unites us with things that cannot be spoken or known, in a union above all the power and capacity of our reasoned thinking or intellectual understanding."[80] We should "dare not say or think anything of the super-autonomous (ὑπερουσίου) and hidden Godhead that is not revealed to us by God in Holy Scripture."[81]

His words here and in many other places that stress in ever new ways God's ineffability, inconceivability, and unnameability could be read to mean that the natural knowledge of God should be totally excluded and that Holy Scripture were the only source of our knowledge of God as far as we can attain it at all. However, we must weigh his every word carefully and compare it with other passages. We must also take into account the procedure the Areopagite actually followed. He warns against "daring" to say anything about God apart from the words of Scripture. A little later he calls for "holy awe brooking no inquiry."[82] Do these words {110} not imply that such inquiry may well be possible in itself but is a dangerous affair?

This reading also accords with the view as we actually find it in Dionysius of the Creator's relationship to creatures. Besides the *major dissimilitudo* [greater unlikeness] he surely allows for a certain *similitudo* [likeness]. And while assuring us on the other hand that no trace leads us to God's hidden infinity, he at once emphasizes that nothing that is lacks all share in the good.[83] But "good" for him is the first of all of God's names.[84] Hence in every be-ing there lies something that makes it apt to serve as a springboard to the "Primal Be-ing," the "Over-Be-ing ," the Good in Person that has called it into existence. This leap is a mental act and it is possible only for enlightened minds. As all being comes from him who is Being Itself and all good comes from him who is Goodness Itself, so all enlightenment [comes] from him who is Light Itself. God allots to created minds the measure of enlightenment in accord with their capacity to understand. Beyond this measure they ought not to aspire; otherwise they will plunge into the depths.

The question whether there is natural knowledge of God now comes down to whether there is a "natural light," that is, a light proper to the nature of the created mind that lets it find its way from creature to Creator without any special enlightenment or whether it needs a separate enlightenment for the purpose. According to Dionysius the brilliance of divine light illuminates us in Holy Scripture. We are taught to see this light through the holy songs prompted by Holy Scripture itself (that is, through the church's liturgy). This is how we become able to grasp and praise God:

> as far as he himself has told us about himself in Holy Scripture. For instance, that he is the cause of all things, their origin, their being and life. He is the calling back and raising again of those who have fallen away, the reshaping and restoring of those who have effaced the divine image in themselves.... He is security for those who stand, light of the enlightened, the source of completion and perfection of the perfect.... "[85]

{111} Besides the mysteries of faith proper, these examples include a fact that in Thomas's and the Church's view is accessible to natural knowledge: God is the cause of all things.

The Areopagite is obviously not making any fundamental distinction here between the objects of natural and supernatural knowledge of God. Must we take his words to mean that without the help of Holy Scripture and the hierarchy [86] our mind cannot raise itself to the divine at all? Dionysius seems to have thought that there is no other insurance against dangerous errors. He cannot mean that it is not possible at all to conceive the notion of a God by purely natural ways. Against this is his distinction mentioned above between symbolic and philosophical theology, as well as the fact that he is teaching in the midst of and taking issue with all kinds of idol worship and heresy. All of them after all have some idea of God and hold some teaching about him. But since they spurn the true light sent to them in various ways, they miss the truth.

How can this view be reconciled with the fact that the Areopagite obviously uses sources other than Holy Scripture, tradition, and saintly authors who themselves built upon this foundation of Scripture and tradition? When critics discovered that his writings show considerable agreement in content and form with Neoplatonic writers, Proclus especially—in particular the long excursus on evil in the fourth chapter of *De Divinis Nominibus* with Proclus's *De malorum subsistentia* [On the Subsistence of Evils]— they took it as proof of his dishonesty. Many saw his appeal to Holy Scripture and his concealment of the pagan authors he was using as the height of hypocrisy.

We do not think that there are grounds for such indignation. The Dionysian Corpus as a whole treats of God's revelation and would lead {112} people to understand revelation and thereby guide them on their way to God. Holy Scripture takes the lead here, but Scripture itself needs exegesis. And in his exegetical work the Areopagite does not spurn the aids offered him in the intellectual world of contemporary philosophy familiar to him and to his readers, indeed even in non-Christian religious doctrines and cults. But if he, outside Holy Scripture and ecclesiastical.... [87]

[*Symbolism*]

...no longer sensible but invisible and spiritual.

The word "image" already implies genuine referrings, not signs arbitrarily tacked on without any objective foundation. After all, for something to be recognized as an image, it must have something in common with what it depicts, as Dionysius says of fire.[88]

On the other hand these referrings must not be as absolutely compelling as those that lead further within the world of senses. How else would it be possible for so many to "have eyes yet see not, have ears and hear not"? How could the same language that reveals divine truth to one be at the same time a veil concealing it from another?

A whole series of questions are interlinked here. "Symbolic theology" as picture-language or image-language of God and the things of God presupposes first a definite relationship between the sensible and non-sensible world ("non-sensible world" may be taken for many different things). On the other hand it presupposes a definite frame of mind in those who use this language in speaking or understanding.

The non-sensible world can be understood first as the "natural-intellectual." Here "nature" is not taken in the modern sense as the object of natural science, the world of corporeal things extended in space, in contrast to "spirit." It rather has the sense in which Aristotle speaks {113} of "φύσις" and the scholastics of *natura:* the basis, interior and proper to a thing, for its characteristic being and activity in contrast to "supernature" or "grace." The natural-intellectual world—I mean the world of personal goods, of "meaning" and of the values of spirit—is experienced naturally, that is, with the cognitive powers set in the nature of created minds. The supernatural may immediately be grasped only when nature is elevated and enlightened by grace.

{Dionysius himself gives an example of symbolic speech in the area of natural experience (in order to clarify the way "symbolic theology" expresses things). We may think of the soul, he says, as a kind of bodily form and attribute parts to it, although it is actually indivisible. Its "parts" should then be understood differently from those of corporeal things. The mind's knowing power would be called the head, opinion the neck (since it lies midway between the rational and the irrational), and so forth. That is, the names of the parts of the body would be used symbolically as symbols for the faculties of the soul. (Similarly he says we could speak of God's breadth, length, and depth to suggest his going forth to all things, his power ranging over everything and his hiddenness and unknowability, which no be-ing may grasp.[89]}*

It is clear that in this case—just as with the mixing bowl—there is no image relation proper. There may well be a certain objective commonness between what the words immediately express—hence it is more than a sign-relation only arbitrarily established—but the way it expresses things is not drawn from intuition, and thus it is

---

* {This passage was crossed out by Edith Stein.—Ed.}

not understandable either merely on the basis of intuition. Its manner of expression is founded upon a reasoned comparison and its meaning must be "guessed at" or explained.

What we have here is "allegory," today distinguished from "symbol," which is the "meaning-*picture*" [*Sinn-Bild*] in the proper sense. Holy Scripture is rich in allegorical figures and the exegesis {114} of the Fathers as well as the rabbinical exegesis before it is rich in allegorical interpretation. Dionysius *also* deals with allegorical speech under "symbolic theology," but this is not all he means by it. Such is clear from what he says about fire, which he takes to be a genuine symbol. Spatial dimensions, too, have some genuine symbolic value in relation to the divine—only, the particular interpretation that the Areopagite gives them is not to be gotten from them immediately and intuitively, but it has an allegorical character.

We may claim in general that symbol-relations form the objective basis for allegorical language and its interpretation. It would not be possible to "produce" designations between the visible and invisible unless the visible of itself pointed beyond itself, [and] the invisible had features that were reflected in the visible. We would not think of bestowing the names of bodily parts on the powers of the soul unless the body spoke a "language" testifying in the most diverse ways to things of the soul (we will come back to this shortly), and unless it also showed a ranking in its structure corresponding to a parallel order in the soul. Divine teaching could not be compared with food and drink if it were not proper to it to enter into the soul and build it up and to be more easily and better absorbed by some in one way and by others in another.

Symbolic relations need not generally and necessarily rely on allegorical analysis. They can be understood in themselves and can find a "natural expression." Thus for example we speak of "burning" zeal and "hot" desire. Allegorical interpretation is indicated when from what we intuit there speaks a range of meaning that admits different (but not mutually exclusive) conceptions. Allegory then fixes the meaning in a certain direction and because of its very unambiguity causes an impoverishment.

All of sensible nature speaks a symbolic language. If convention as it were has dubbed the lily the symbol of purity and the violet the symbol of modesty, we have here allegories that are already sketched out {115} in the intuitive character of these flowers and should be readily understood on this basis. But from the "face" of the flowers something else "speaks" to us that in popular allegories is not in evidence. And not everything that speaks to us therefrom can be expressed at all in words. In "nature symbolism" we meet something that is able to unlock for us a more restricted and proper meaning of "symbol." The general meaning was that of some sensible thing serving as a "meaning-picture" of something non-sensible and providing linguistic expression for it. The examples above have to do mostly with two known things that could come into this relation for the sake of a certain objective commonness. Zeal we can call "burning" because we know by experience what zeal is and what in it we style "burning." We also know modesty and what makes it resemble the violet.

The symbolic relation, however, does not necessarily presuppose that the two things bearing the relation are known. Actually the meaning of symbol is perhaps most properly fulfilled when what we know leads us to something we do not know. In a way the symbolism of the human body is like this. Its whole external appearance points beyond itself to something disclosed thereby. All knowledge of ontic being and living is essentially built upon it.

Without "expression" we would have no access to the being of someone else's soul. And while the inner experience of the being of our own soul contributes essentially to how we understand the phenomena of expression, our experience of ourselves depends in turn upon our experience of the other. The experience of the being of the soul develops on the sensible and intellectual levels in the mutual dependence of the experience of the self and the experience of the other. Conceiving a body in its physical aspect [*Körper*] as human [*Leib*] means regarding everything about its shape and movement as "expression," taking everything "outside" as a symbol of something "inside." The symbol, "meaning-picture," is understood in this way. What is perceived on the outside (facial features, expressions and the like) points beyond itself to something quite different and yet has something in common with it that makes the expression-relation possible and enables the expression to be understood.

One of the characteristics of this relationship {116} is that the unknown becomes accessible through the known without our having to know the relationship between them beforehand. In order to recognize someone represented in a portrait, we must know the person represented. But we may become acquainted with someone we do not know through his portrait. And we can "tell by looking" at a good portrait that it is a *portrait* (not just a fanciful creation) and that it is a *good* portrait. Of course not everyone can do this. The eye must be trained for it and exercised. The image-language of bodily expression, too, must be first learned a little at a time (actually, so must sense perception). Nor does everyone learn it equally well; there are folks who

{are especially cut out for it and develop it further than others. But all this remains within the realm of the natural.

It could be used as an example of how we grasp symbols and understand *language* in the proper and narrower sense. But the structure of language is too complicated to be considered within this narrow framework. Similarly, we can only note how indispensable symbolic knowledge is for any aesthetic view of the world as well as for the creation, understanding, and enjoyment of works of art.}*

[*Symbols and God*]

Because human knowledge advances from the sensible to the spiritual [*geistig*] with the help of symbolic connections, it is natural for human language to transfer the names of sensible things and events to the spiritual: we speak of "overflowing" joy, "dark" fate, "blazing" anger. The more natural our language and the more concrete our thinking, the more vividly we feel these connections.

Now, how is it possible for us, starting with the things of experience, to reach something lying beyond all experience? When the church and her holy doctors speak of the natural knowledge of God, they are thinking of our understanding as it reasons from effects to a first cause and from the purposeful and lawful order of the universe to a being that orders it by bestowing purpose and law.

This, however, is not what symbolic {117} theology is all about. When Moses calls God a consuming fire, his designation neither rests on a deduction of natural reasoning nor intends to prompt such a process. He "experienced" God, stood before him, was seized by

---

* {This passage was crossed out by Edith Stein.—Ed.}

him. And only through this image could he convey what he then experienced. He who "knows" God will understand (as we recognize someone we know in a portrait or in a "typical" tale told about him). One who does not know God, I mean one has not come into such immediate contact with him, can come to know him as we become acquainted with a stranger through a good portrait or the description of a typical feature.

Several sorts of understanding are of course presupposed here. To get to know people from pictures we must "know all about pictures" and "know all about people." To meet God through a symbolic expression we must have an eye for those referrings that point from this world into a world "beyond." And we must have a certain appreciation for what is meant by "God." (Incidentally, both types of understanding are also required to be able to work out arguments for God's existence and to understand them.)

Are these presuppositions "natural" or a gift of grace? Holy Scripture calls one who denies God a "fool" ("*dixit insipiens in corde suo: 'non est Deus'* [the fool said in his heart: 'there is no God']")[90] This seems to mean that a man of sound mind recognizes God's existence, that to deny it is abnormal. And when the Epistle to the Romans says (1:20) that the invisible in God has been intellectually knowable from his works since the creation of the world, we take it as referring to this pointing of the visible beyond itself as a natural revelation of God to the human mind as such. According to this there would be no need to be raised above nature to get beyond the visible world, but rather to sink down below nature to understand no more the language of the visible world pointing "beyond."

[Atheism and theism]

The fact that millions of people {118} are "atheists" does not speak against this.[91] "Atheism" should perhaps be taken in quite different senses with different people. If it means the denial of God's existence, the denier must attach a meaning to the word "God"—indeed, in keeping with his claim, the same meaning that the faithful give it, since what they believe is of course what he wishes to deny.

What is his claim based upon? The atheist may have had faith and may still recall what "God" used to mean for him. But how did he arrive at his understanding originally? Probably from a religious upbringing. He heard about God at home and in school and accepted it without a second thought, as we take so many other things for granted without being convinced from our own intuition.

However, we should bear in mind that our understanding of language takes shape hand in hand with our experience and with all our intellectual holdings. To learn from "hearsay" about something we do not know we need some access to it from the sensible and intellectual world that we do know. Otherwise the words will remain meaningless to us. The atheist may say that God was depicted to him as a very large, strong man, much larger and stronger than all others; and he could imagine this sort of thing as we can picture mountains that are much higher than all those we know. When he rejects this "god," we must tell him that is not denying what we understand by "God." But if he says that "God" means the same thing to him as it does to us, then we, too, should assume a common basis for understanding.

Certainly for most children human ideas are a bridge to thoughts about God. But they go beyond to the "totally other," other than anything their experience encounters or can encounter in the world. And this they allow to move them to accept the teaching of supernatural {119} revelation as the fulfillment of what they at first grasped in but empty fashion as the "totally other," and as the answer to the riddles that experience itself poses without ever being able to solve them. In this case passing from the world of natural experience into the world of supernatural faith comes about as a matter of course and almost imperceptibly.

The acceptance of faith is nonetheless "free"; the possibility of rejecting it remains. But rejection and acceptance are not of quite equal weight: while the initial acceptance of faith in its "normal" unfolding usually takes place smoothly, more often than not the rejection of faith represents a sharp break or "turning away." Its opposite movement, the equally free and conscious acceptance of faith, is "conversion."

The lack of faith is the state that lies between the two. It may even come first in individuals who from the beginning of their lives grow up in an atmosphere of unbelief. The person who freely chooses not to believe will not only reject the teaching of a revealed religion, he will also refuse to believe the referrings within natural experience itself. If it is possible to practice abstention in regard to sense perception and leave open the question whether what it sets before our eyes really exists, it is all the more possible in regard to the referrings that after all can never come to fulfillment within natural experience.

Practiced with persistence this abstention can become habitual and turn into a state of blindness where the referrings are no longer regarded at all. One so blinded, in fact, no longer sees beyond "this world" and now "can" no longer believe what he is told about a world "beyond." (This "cannot" is not quite right; he could still perhaps believe, but to do so he would have to use force and set himself against the world as he actually now sees it.) Arguments for the existence of the world beyond no longer make sense to him. Nor can he understand any more the language that reports on experiences in that world. From him the words of "symbolic theology" actually veil what they unveil to others.

[*Speaking about God*]

In contrast, in the "normal," uncurtailed, natural {120} experience, we have something that makes it possible at the same time to follow and accept arguments for God's existence, to accept a revealed faith, and to understand symbolic theology.[92]

Parallel to these possibilities are three different ways of "speaking about God" that address different audiences and have different aims.

Arguments for God's existence belong to "natural theology." Through them the teacher's natural understanding engages the natural understanding of his hearers to afford them the means to parry and dispel possible doubts against faith stemming from reason. It is assumed that the hearers are bothered or threatened by doubts or else they have the duty to assist others in their trials of faith. The simple faithful do not need them.

Preaching of the faith is based upon divine revelation and has the mission of spreading what God has revealed about himself throughout the "whole world." It aims at the general acceptance of the faith and at a way of life in accord with its requirements.

Symbolic theology is but an excerpt from the total content of revelation; more precisely, it is the *symbolic intimation of an experience in a new meaning*—a mysterious contact with the supernatural world. Revelation as a whole includes much that, although in fact communicated by God's word, is in itself accessible to natural knowledge and is grasped by natural reason even by those who accept it as a teaching of faith: for example, things relating to the moral and social order.[93]

{121} {Symbolic theology, however, is intended for a select circle and intends more than instructing its members in the faith: it would raise up further those who are striving for holiness (since they have already experienced a higher enlightenment). Through its images it unveils mysteries of a suprasensible world for them. Through these images it would help them to free themselves from the sensible world more and more and bring them to the point where they no longer have need of sensible images at all.}*

We mentioned that someone may already have a certain understanding of these images without having the particular experience himself, just as he can understand the writings of the mystics without himself being a mystic. The person who has already accepted in faith that there is a God and a suprasensible world beyond the world of experience—I mean, effects stemming from God and spirits that experience and pass on these effects, and also launch effects of their own—will understand that an experiential contact with that world is also possible, and he will be eager to grasp whatever the images can convey to him.

This person's idea will none the less be empty and unintuitive as long as he lacks experiences of his own, and it will be easily dulled by misunderstandings and illusions, especially when a lively imagination seeks to make up for the lack of intuition. Still, this unsatisfactory understanding may be just the incentive he needs to do what will enable him to move ahead to a fuller understanding.

---

* {This passage was crossed out by Edith Stein.—Ed.}

[*Faith*]

On the other hand we should bear in mind that the believer is already "enlightened," that faith is a "supernatural light." Hence here we are no longer standing on the step of purely natural experience, and we must go down to it once again. Lacking faith—I mean having yet to accept revealed truth—is not after all the same thing as being blind and deaf to the message of faith, as is the person hardened in unbelief and, in the extreme case, the atheist on principle.

"Undogmatic {122} faith" comes in many varieties and may be a patchwork of all sorts of scraps, usually, it would seem, taken ultimately from thinly veiled revealed sources. Such "faith" may be unbiased and open to enrichment and transformation. But for it to turn into genuine, full, supernatural faith, it will always need, besides the free decision to accept it, an inpouring of that characteristic "dark light" which belongs to faith essentially ("dark" relative to the clear insight of understanding).

But this enlightenment need not come before we understand image language. It is possible that the very images of symbolic theology evoke the enlightenment, and that its making facts that witness to a higher effectiveness intuitable for us may awaken faith in a higher reality. Clearly, from such faith springs the desire to come into personal contact with this higher world now. This is precisely the aim of symbolic theology. It would be a *cheirogogia*,[94] a "leading by the hand." Through the mediumship of a sense expression, one mind speaks to another in order to lead it into a spiritual realm and to form it therefrom into a purely spiritual understanding.

[*Summary*]

How this forming process is possible we will not discuss here. We must be content to point out how *symbolic theology* should be interpreted as a *way to know God*, and that now seems to have been fairly settled: symbolic theology is speaking about God in images taken from the world of sense. What it expresses is a direct experience that the person gains when he himself is seized by God.

Symbolic theology thus addresses creatures of sensitive-intellectual nature who are still so closely attached to the sensible that they need the mediation of sense images, but are capable in principle of a purely spiritual understanding and of a personal experience of supernatural effects. Understanding images presupposes {123} an objective commonness between the sense world and the spiritual, divine world. It further assumes that the understanding person either already has faith in a supernatural world or that he has an unbiased and uncurtailed view of the natural world with all its referrings, and at the same time that he is open to a message from that supernatural world and can pass over into faith. The *goal* of this lowest step of positive theology is to pave the way for a purely spiritual knowledge of God, and beyond this, for an immediate experience of one's own, and finally for union with God.

II

[*The Second Way to Know God*]

The *second way to know God* is set forth in the *De divinis nominibus*: the *interpretation of the spiritual names of God.* Now we need not rely upon a few fragments, but have the entire writing at our disposal, the most substantial of the writings that have come down to us from Dionysius. We cannot of course cover the whole content of the great work within these narrow bounds; we must be content to give an excerpt in order to bring out the characteristics of this way of knowledge.

In his introductory chapter, as we mentioned, the Areopagite deems it presumptuous to wish to say anything about God independently of Holy Scripture. Moreover he insists, very emphatically and in the all sorts of ways, that even the spiritual names of God are unable to grasp the ungraspable. But God has imparted a reflection of his goodness to every creature. And to spirits that do not presume to aspire to what is not intended for them but in holy reverence, composure, and pious awe stand ready for what God would grant them, to these he gives illumination in proportion to their ability to comprehend.[95]

When we consider the names that Holy Scripture has coined
{124} for God, we find that almost all are founded upon the effects
of his divine goodness. He is called *one* in virtue of the unity by
which we are one and are led to a godlike unity. He is *wise* and
beautiful, because all things, if they keep their nature intact, are full
of divine harmony and holy beauty, etc.[96]

Thus it is proper for him who is the Cause of all things and is
above all things to have no names, yet at the same time to have all
names of all things. He is fittingly named after all things, since he
has anticipated everything in a simple, unbounded manner
through the perfect goodness in his Providence that brings everything about.[97] While being and remaining *one*—in a sense of "oneness" going beyond anything we have access to—he nonetheless
sets forth a multiplicity from himself and this is why he can be
grasped.

God's "procession" should be taken in several ways. In his second chapter Dionysius treats processions in the exclusive sense,
those within the Godhead through which the *one* divine being
[*Wesen*] unfolds in three Persons. The divine names here treated
are based on the outward procession of the Godhead as a whole in
the works of creation.

Dionysius recognizes a twofold multiplicity mediating between
the one God and the diversity of the sense world: the world of
created pure spirits—the "celestial hierarchy"—and the world of
pure "ideas" or "essences," from which the names of God are
taken.[98] It was mentioned in the beginning that the heavenly spirits,
too, play a key role in our knowledge of God. But this is not the
question here; it rather concerns that impersonal, {125} intermediate
realm. They are treated in this work only insofar as they, the highest of
all creatures, along with everything created, have the origin of their
being in the first One, the "Primal Be-ing," "Over-Be-ing."[99]
Dionysius does not appeal to Plato, but it is precisely in this work
that the Platonist is unmistakable.[100]

The first divine name he considers —the one most properly
applying to the divine essence— is *good.* As *goodness* itself, the good
in itself, good by its very being, it radiates goodness to all be-ings,
as the sun illuminates everything receptive in some way to its light,
by merely being, not in virtue of some thought or intent. (The sun,

however, is to the good only as a poor copy is to the original.) To the good every be-ing—from the highest spirits to be-ings lacking reason and life—owes its being and all that it is, its ranking and conformity to law, its share in the good and its tending toward the good. For as in the visible realm everything makes for the light, so every be-ing strives after the good, each in its very own way. But to the highest spirits it is especially proper to radiate back the divine good and turn toward the good what is subordinate to it. Thus the good, as bound up with being, stands above all be-ing, and, as bound up with being, it is at the same time bound up with form whereby the formless is formed.

The platonic purport is perhaps more clearly in evidence in Dionysius's explanation of the *beautiful*.[101] The good as such is also called "the beautiful" or "beauty." The two—the beautiful and beauty—should not be separated in the oneness of the all-embracing Cause, while in be-ings what shares in beauty is called "beautiful" and what all things beautiful share in is called "beauty."

Supraessential {126} beauty is called *beauty* as that which bestows an appropriate beauty on all things, elicits all harmony and all splendor in them, and calls[102] and turns everything to itself as to the light.

But it is called *beautiful* as the wholly beautiful, over-beautiful, as what is beautiful ever and in the same way, neither coming to be nor passing away, neither increasing nor decreasing, not partly beautiful and partly ugly or for many beautiful but at times unbeautiful, not beautiful with respect to this and ugly with respect to that, not beautiful here but not there; not beautiful for some but not for others. It is rather so called as that which is always uniformly beautiful in itself and in harmony with itself, as that which possesses in itself, overabundantly and beforehand, the original beauty of all that is beautiful.

For all beauty and all that is beautiful subsists beforehand simply in the simple and supernatural nature of everything beautiful. All things are beautiful in virtue of this, the beautiful, for it is the ground of the being of all things. All harmony and all commonness of be-ings subsists through it, for it guides everything to itself through love and unifies everything in this striving. It sets everything in motion and is the goal for whose sake everything comes to be.

Just for this reason the beautiful and the good are the same: what everything strives for and what everything shares in.

Now, that which suffers not the good to abide in itself but stirs it in an excess that brings forth all things and puts it to work is *Love*.[103] For love is "ecstatic" and makes the lover the possession of the beloved, as Paul says: "no longer I live but Christ lives in me."[104]

And so we might even be so bold as to say that the Author of all things has been beside himself in the exuberance of his loving goodness: he goes out of himself without going out of himself and through his Providence cares for every be-ing.[105]

But he is called not only "Love," {127} but "Beloved" as well. For in the creature he brings forth love for himself. As Love he bestirs himself, as the Beloved he bestirs creatures toward himself. Therein the divine love proves beginningless and endless, an everlasting cycle, wheeling, but for the sake of the good, from the good, in the good, toward the good.[106]

Notes

1. John Paul II, *Fides et Ratio: Encyclical Letter on the Relationship between Faith and Reason* (Boston: Pauline Books and Media, 1998), par. 74.
2. Ibid.
3. See Marianne Sawicki, *Body, Text, and Science: The Literacy of Investigative Practices and the Phenomenology of Edith Stein* (Dordrecht: Kluwer Academic Publishers, 1997), 189. Sawicki refers readers to "editor's note 5 for Stein's letter to Roman Ingarden of 1 November 1928," found in Edith Stein, *Briefe an Roman Ingarden 1917–1939*, vol. 14 of *Edith Steins Werke* (Freiburg: Herder, 1991).
4. See p. xxii below.
5. The extensive Marvin Farber collection in the archives of the State University of New York at Buffalo includes over 80 boxes of material, divided into two overlapping categories. The boxes listed under "22/5F/768" contain correspondence and papers on phenomenology and philosophy in general. The boxes listed under "22/5F/769" contain letters mainly connected with the *Journal of Philosophy and Phenomenological Research,* of which Farber was the editor for many years. Archivist Christopher Densmore helped to locate the materials cited here.
6. Stein to Farber, 4 April 1940, Farber series 22/5F/768, box 22–20. The translation of these previously unpublished Stein letters in the Buffalo archives is by Sr. Josephine Koeppel, O.C.D. These four letters will appear in the revised German edition of Edith Stein's letters, forthcoming.
7. Farber to Kaufmann, 3 March 1940, Farber series 22/5F/768, box 11–2. This letter is apparently misdated, since it seems to refer back to Stein's letter of 4 April 1940, and since the reply

of Kaufmann (who typically responded quickly to Farber's missives) is dated May 7. (Farber elsewhere misdates letters, and perhaps in this case he meant to write "May" instead of "March.")

8. Kaufmann to Farber, 7 May 1940, Farber series 22/5F/768, box 11–2.
9. Farber to Stein, Farber series 22/5F/768, box 22–20.
10. Stein to Farber, 4 November 1940, Farber series 22/5F/768, box 22–20.
11. Stein to Farber, 4 April 1941, Farber series 22/5F/768, box 22–20.
12. Farber to Stein, 9 May 1941, Farber series 22/5F/768, box 22–20.
13. Stein to Farber, 12 September 1941, Farber series 22/5F/768, box 22–20.
14. Farber to Stein, 25 October 1941, Farber series 22/5F/768, box 22–20.
15. Kaufmann to Farber, 7 November 1941, Farber series 22/5F/768, box 11–3.
16. Schütz to Farber, 3 May 1942, Farber series 22/5F/768, box 20–18.
17. Farber to Schütz, 9 May 1942, Farber series 22/5F/768, box 20–18.
18. Kaufmann to Farber, 19 June 1942, Farber series 22/5F/768, box 11–3.
19. Kaufmann to Farber, 30 March 1944, Farber series 22/5F/768, box 11–5.
20. Farber to Kaufmann, 6 April 1944, Farber series 22/5F/768, box 11–5.
21. Allers to Farber, 5 September 1945, Farber series 22/5F/768, box 1–5.
22. Allers to Farber, 9 October 1945, Farber series 22/5F/768, box 1–5.
23. Sister Theresia Benedicta a Cruce, O.C.D., "Ways to Know God: The 'Symbolic Theology' of Dionysius the Areopagite and Its Factual Presuppositions," trans. Rudolf Allers, *The Thomist* 9 (July, 1946), 379. Oddly, Dr. Gelber does not draw upon the evidence in the correspondence she herself edited, where Edith Stein explains to Mother Petra Brüning, on 13 June 1941:

"I do not know whether I wrote to you that as part of my new duties I am to write a short preliminary study as a contribution to the periodical *Philosophy and Phenomenological Research,* which has been published since last year by some Husserl disciples at the University of Buffalo, NY. This minor work ("Ways to Know God: The 'Symbolic Theology' of the Areopagite and Its Factual Presuppositions") is at present being typed by Ruth K. (Kantorowicz)." See Edith Stein, *Self-Portrait in Letters, 1916–1942,* trans. Josephine Koeppel (Washington, DC: ICS Publications, 1993), letter no. 321. Cf. letter no. 326.

24. See pages xxiv of the "Editor's Introduction."

25. Edith Stein Center, ed., *Edith Stein: A Biographical Essay and Ways to Know God, by Sister Teresia Benedicta of the Cross, OCD* (New York: Edith Stein Guild Publications, 1981).

26. John Paul II, *Fides et Ratio,* par. 74.

Editor's Introduction

1. [See "Foreword to the ICS Edition" for more recent information on the history of this essay.—Trans.]

2. [The Archivum Carmelitanum Edith Stein was recently moved to Würzburg, Germany.—Trans.]

3. [See "Foreword to the ICS Edition" for more recent information on the history of this essay.—Trans.]

4. [*The Thomist* is currently published by the Dominicans at The Thomist Press, 487 Michigan Avenue, N.E., Washington, D.C. 20017.—Trans.]

Husserl and Aquinas: A Comparison

1. As the title indicates, this is but an initial attempt. It is limited first by the space available. A proper treatment would require a thorough account of phenomenology in all its areas and throughout its various stages of development, as well as an equally thorough description of St. Thomas's philosophy (I purposely avoid the term "Thomism" since I base my comparison not on any traditional scholastic system but on an

overview drawn from Thomas's writings.) This is not the place for such an undertaking, and even now I would not be sufficiently prepared for it. However, to sketch the spirit of the two philosophies here and there in a few essential lines as they have suggested themselves in my reading of Thomas heretofore—this I do feel I may now attempt.

2. [*Logische Untersuchungen/Prolegomena zur reinen Logik* (Logical Studies/Prologomena to Pure Logic), 1900–1901.—Trans.]

3. The view given here essentially follows the *Quaestiones Disputatae de Veritate* to be published this year by Herder as *Untersuchungen über die Wahrheit*. [Stein is here referring to her two-volume German translation of Thomas Aquinas's *Quaestiones Disputatae de Veritate*, published in Breslau by Borgmeyer in 1931–1932, and later reprinted as volumes III and IV of *Edith Steins Werke*.—Trans.]

4. [*Ideen zu einer reinen Phänomenologie und phänomenologischen Philosophie* (Ideas for a Pure Phenomenology and Phenomenological Philosophy), the leading article of the first issue of the *Jahrbuch für Philosophie und Phänomenologische Forschung*, 1913; English translation, *Ideas*, by W. R. Boyce Gibson, 1931.—Trans.]

5. [The text has "you" (the word was not changed from the dialogue version).—Trans.]

KNOWLEDGE, TRUTH, BEING

1. "To be know*able*" in the case of God is meaningless outside of a relation to a finite knowing mind.

ACTUAL AND IDEAL BEING, SPECIES, TYPE AND IMAGE

1. "Quidditas creari dicitur: quia antequam esse habeat, nihil est nisi forte in intellectu creantis, ubi non est creatura, sed creatrix essentia," *De Potentia*, question 3, article 5, ad 2.

2. Aquinas, *De Veritate*, question 3, art. 1. See *Untersuchung über die Wahrheit*, in *Edith Steins Werke*, vol. 3, pp. 89ff. [St. Thomas

wrote: "Dicitur forma alicujus illud ad quod aliquid formatur; et haec est forma exemplaris ad cujus similitudinem aliquid constituitur."—Trans.]

3. Ibid., p. 94. [St. Thomas wrote: "Haec ergo videtur esse ratio ideae, quod idea sit forma quam aliquid imitatur ex intentione agentis."—Trans.]

4. Ibid., p. 95. [St. Thomas wrote: "Non est autem conveniens ponere Deum agere propter finem alium a se et accipere aliunde unde sit sufficiens ad agendum; ideo non possumus ponere ideas esse extra Deum, sed in mente divina tantum." —Trans.]

SKETCH OF A FOREWORD TO *FINITE AND ETERNAL BEING*

1. *Untersuchungen über die Wahrheit* (Breslau: Verlag Borgmeyer, 1931 [vol. 1], 1932 [vol. 2], and Latin-German glossary [1935]). [See *Edith Steins Werke,* volumes III and IV.—Ed.]

2. "Husserls Phänomenologie und die Philosophie des hl. Thomas von Aquino" (Halle: Verlag Niemeyer, 1929). [This is the first selection in this volume.—Trans.]

WAYS TO KNOW GOD

1. [Manuscript I₁ and I₂.—Ed.]

2. Letter 7, par. 2, in Migne, *Patrologia Graeca* [PG] 3:1081f. and *De divinis nominibus,* ch. 3, par. 2, PG 3:681ff.

3. Acts 17:33f.

4. Especially noteworthy are the works of P. S. Stiglmayr and H. Koch, cited by O. Bardenhewer, *Geschichte der altchristlichen Literatur,* Freiburg i. Br., 1924, vol. 4.

5. Cf. PG 4:21–22 in the prologue of Maximus the Confessor.

6. I refer to Hugo Ball, "Dionysius Areopagita" in *Byzantinisches Christentum. Drei Heiligenleben,* pp. 61ff., Munich and Leipzig, 1923.

7. It is the merit of P. G. Théry, O.P., whose works are models of precision, to have brought out these facts. Cf. *Études Dionysiennes, Hilduin Traducteur de Denys* (Paris: Yini) vol. 1, 1932; vol. 2, 1937.

The second volume contains the text of Hilduin's translation, the first Latin version of Dionysius.

8. [*Opera*], Borgnet edition, Paris, 1892 [*Commentaria in Dionysium*, vol. 14, p. 1].
9. Ecclesiastes 1:7.
10. "ὁ πᾶς τῶν ὑποχειμένων ἱερῶν λόγος," *Ecclesiastica Hierarchia*, ch. 1, par. 3, PG 3:373.
11. This image is taken from Moses' ascent of the holy mountain (Exodus 19), which the Areopagite, following the tradition of the Fathers, interprets in the mystical sense (*Mystical Theology*, ch. 1, par. 3, PG 3:969ff.).
12. "Positive" contrasts here with "negative" theology, not as today with "natural" or "speculative" theology.
13. This writing is lost. Critics do not believe that it ever existed, any more than the other [works] that he mentions which have not been preserved. Cf. Hugo Koch, "Der pseudepigraphische Charakter der dionysischen Schriften" in *Theologische Quartalschrift*, Tübingen, 77 (1895): 362ff.
14. Scheeben, *Dogmatik* (Freiburg i. Br., 1873), vol. 1, 423, calls it the "richest work from the Patristic period treating *ex professo* the entire doctrine *de Deo uno* [on the one God] (his judgment refers to the *Divine Names* plus the commentary of Maximus the Confessor).
15. PG 3:635ff.
16. PG 3:135ff and 325ff.
17. Ibid., 1103ff.
18. Ibid., 913f. [*The Thomist* adds here: "If one were not to limit the meaning of 'theology' to words, but to extend it to all kinds of discussion of things Divine, one would have to take account of the whole treatise on *Ecclesiastical Hierarchy;* to make use of the narrower sense appears, however, advisable, if only for external reasons."—Trans.]
19. Ibid., 327–328.
20. Ibid., 1033–1034.
21. Ibid., 1047–1048.
22. Cf. Aristotle, *Metaphysics*, and Thomas Aquinas, *De veritate* [On Truth] ques. 9, art. 1, and ques. 10, art. 1 ad 1 *in contra*. The "major dissimilitudo" also appears in the same passage. [See Stein's translation in *Untersuchungen über die Wahrheit*, vol. 1

(Breslau: Verlag Borgmeyer, 1931), 27; *Edith Steins Werke*, vol. 3, p. 223ff., 240.—Ed.]

23. PG 3:1103ff. The Areopagite's "letters" should probably be regarded not as letters in the proper sense but as short, informal treatises, that are useful for supplementing the major writings.

24. Ibid. par. 1.

25. Romans 1:20 seems to be meant.

26. Deuteronomy 4:11ff. and 24.

27. Psalm 17:31.

28. Ch. 15, par. 2, PG 3:327.

29. Wisdom 7:22ff.

30. Proverbs 9:2ff. says that wisdom mixes her wine but does not mention the bowl itself.

31. Ibid., par. 3 (PG 1109f.).

32. Ibid., par. 4.

33. Ibid., par. 5.

34. Reading *unmitteilbar* (Dionysius's ἀκοινώνητον) for *unmittelbar* in manuscript (cf. footnote 31 in *The Thomist*).

35. Ibid., par. 6.

36. *De divinis nominibus*, ch. 9, par. 5, PG 3:913f.

37. Ch. 3, PG 3:1053.

38. ...τίνες αἱ ἀπὸ τῶν αἰσθητῶν ἐπὶ τὰ θεῖα μετωνυμίαι.

39. E.g., *De ecclesiastica hierarchia* [On the Ecclesiastical Hierarchy], ch. 5, par. 5; PG 3:505f.

40. Ibid., ch. 4, par. 4; PG 3:535f.

41. *Mystical Theology*, ch. 3, PG 3:1053f.

42. Coining compound words like θεοτυπία and ἱερόπλαστοι is another characteristic of the Areopagite's style. Translating them is always a risky and makeshift if unavoidable undertaking. τύπος is "type" [*Vorbild*] in the sense in which we speak of the figures, foreshadowings, of Christ in the Old Testament, not as archetype [*Urbild*], but rather as the improper through which the proper is heralded.

43. [The literal sense of Greek συμβάλλειν (*sym-ballein*), underlying "symbol."—Trans.]

44. Deuteronomy 4:24.

45. The Holy Spirit could more properly be so called; he guides the theologian and has him find the words and images, if he does not actually first speak the words to him and show him the images.

46. The heading includes many different kinds.
47. To judge from his words it seems to me hard to say whether he even held natural knowledge of God to be possible at all. (His actual way of proceeding is something else.) In most passages, although he does not call it downright impossible, he sounds as if he at least wants to exclude it as dangerous. (Compare *Mystical Theology* ch. 1, par. 2, PG 3:999f, "On the Divine Names" ch. 1, par. 1, PG 3:585ff.) The distinction he draws in his ninth letter to Titus (PG 3:1106) between a "public, easily understandable" theology proceeding by "philosophical demonstration" and a "secret, veiled" theology parallels the different procedures that he adopts in the "Symbolic Theology" and in his treatment of God's *spiritual* names. Contemporary theology ascribes *both* ways to "natural theology" (cf. Scheeben, *Dogmatik*, vol. 1, p. 482). This is a Thomistic point of view, but I do not know if it is possible to read Dionysius in this sense.
48. ["*Wirklich*" means "real" or "actual" today, but formerly in Middle High German "working," "active," "effective."—Trans.]
49. When biology and psychology proceed "exactly," that is, in accordance with mathematical natural science, they grasp life and soul through their physiological conditions or effects. This is not our concern here. The body may indeed be an approach in our present context, but not as the "physiological" [*Körper*], but the "living" [*Leib*] body, where we can "tell by looking" that it is alive and has a soul.
50. Psalm 29:3.
51. [The German is a compound of two words: "from-picture."—Trans.]
52. [Stein uses the English word "belief" here; the German word *Glaube* means both religious faith (Latin *fides*) and belief in general.—Trans.]
53. Psalm 68:6.
54. Psalm 23.
55. Psalm 44:12; 78:21 and 31.
56. John 11:49ff.
57. Isaiah 6.
58. 1 Samuel 3:1ff.

59. We offer this as one, but by no means the only, possible interpretation of the event, and it provides a good intuitive basis for what we wish to show.

60. [Reading *Gotteserfahrung* for *Gotteserkenntnis* (read by translator in *The Thomist*); see note 75 below.—Trans.]

61. This is true both of the atheist and of one who believes in God but not in a revealed "Word of God."

62. This contrast has nothing to do with the distinction between "living" and "dead" faith, that is, between being in or not in the state of grace.

63. [Missing in manuscript.—Ed.]

64. *The Celestial Hierarchy*, PG 3:121, ch. 1, par. 2.

65. *De Veritate*, ques. 13, art. 2, corpus. [See *Untersuchung über die Wahrheit*, IIa (Breslau, 1932); *Edith Steins Werke*, 3: 337ff.—Ed.]

66. [Literally, "...eyes of the profaning looks of ..."; the translator in *The Thomist* read "eyes," and the previous paraphrase of this quote, to which footnote 68 refers, has "images." Cf. Dionysius 140AB, 476B, 1108A, etc.—Trans.]

67. See above section 2, paragraph 1.

68. The church's teaching that the human mind *can* come to know God through its natural powers does not imply that everybody in all circumstances *must* come to this knowledge. When St. Paul (Romans 1:20) declares pagans to be inexcusable because God can be known from creation, we should think not of single individuals but of the *entirety*, wherein the required help in any case has never been lacking. Moreover, he thought them guilty of not coming to the right w*orship* of God (Romans 1:21) despite the *knowledge of God* that was in fact present. But culpable blindness may also be found in individuals. (We will shortly touch on this below.)

69. We have evidence that Dionysius actually had something like this in mind. In his seventh letter (to Polycarp), par. 2, PG 3:1079f., he answers the charge of the sophist Apollophanes that he, Dionysius, unfairly turned the claims of the Greek philosophers against them, with the countercharge that the Greeks sought to use divine wisdom against God. (Of course the particular instance that the Areopagite is referring to here should hardly be taken as a misuse of Holy Scripture, but his

comment may be understood in a general sense: it illustrates
the controversies of a time when pagan and Christian writers
seized weapons from one another.)
70. Matthew 13:3ff.
71. Matthew 13:11.
72. Luke 24:25ff.
73. Dionysius stresses on the one hand that revelation is accorded
us through the angels (*The Celestial Hierarchy* ch. 4, par. 4, PG
3:181f.) and on the other that Christ is the head of both hierarchies and gives a share in the divine life to each in its own way:
to the angels in a purely spiritual way and to men through the
priesthood and liturgical symbols (*The Ecclesiastical Hierarchy*,
ch. 1, par. 1ff., PG 3:369ff.). The mediating office of the angels
retreats into the background here: the highest members of the
hierarchy receive the "holy gift" from God himself, he says, without mentioning the intervention of the angels (ibid. par. 5, PG
3:375f.).
74. Such is probably the Areopagite's intention, although he distinguishes this theology from symbolic theology as "public" from
"secret" (PG 3:1106).
75. Supposing "*Gotteserfahrung*" for "*Gotteserkenntnis*" (see note 60
above).
76. [Cf. the last paragraph of section I.—Trans.].
77. PG, vol. 3, 1106.
78. *Mystical Theology*, ch. 1, par. 2, PG 3:999f.
79. 1 Corinthians 2:4.
80. *De divinis nominibus*, ch. 1, par. 1, PG 3:585ff.
81. See [previous] note.
82. Ibid., I 3, PG III, 589f.
83. Ibid., I 2, PG vol. III, 58[8]f.
84. Ibid. IV, 1, PG vol. 3:693f.
85. Ibid. ch. 1, par. 3, PG 589f.
86. Mention has been made of angels and priests bringing the divine
illumination to men (cf. p. 10 [of manuscript.—Trans.]).
87. [Pages 25–34 of the fragment are missing here.—Ed.]
88. To be sure, in the various expressions considered, the "image"
relationship should be taken in a more and less proper sense
(compare the following pages).

89. *De divinis nominibus*, ch. 9, par. 5, PG 3:913f. [cf. the end of the first section under "Symbolic Theology."—Trans.]
90. Psalm 1:1 and 53:1.
91. What follows is not to be taken as an attempt to argue for God's existence or to refute atheism—both lie outside our scope—but as a way to uncover what the notion of "symbolic theology" presupposes.
92. In our search for this "something" we began as Dionysius did from external perception and experience. As a matter of fact, the immediate inner living experience of our own being and of its relativeness is at least as important. We treated this *inner way to God,* the predominant one in Augustine, in detail in my book *Endliches und ewiges Sein: Versuch eines Aufstiegs zum Sinn des Seins,* which though given to the press several years ago was prevented from appearing by conditions at the time.
93. Cf. p. 27 above. [The page Stein refers to here is missing from the fragment.—Ed.]
94. PG 3:121–122.
95. *De divinis nominibus,* ch. 1, par. 2, PG 3:587ff.
96. Ibid., ch. 1, par. 4, PG 3:589ff.
97. Ibid., ch. 1, par. 7, PG 3:595f.
98. "Εἶδος," the term for the platonic idea, is not frequent in Dionysius. It occurs in the *De divinis nominibus,* ch. 4, par. 10, PG 3:705 in a list without any discussion, and in ch. 13, par. 3, PG 3:979f., as the "predesigned idea" that gives unity to everything united. The second passage suggests that by his "spiritual names of God" he intends what Plato sought to understand by his "ideas."
99. *De divinis nominibus,* ch. 4, par. 1–2, PG 3:693ff.
100. We need not discuss here the much debated question whether he got anything, or what he got, from Plato directly and what he got through the Neoplatonists, especially Proclus.
101. Ibid., ch. 4, par. 7, PG 3:701ff.
102. "καλοῦν" = what "calls" is cognate to "καλόν" = "beautiful."
103. Ibid., ch. 4, par. 10, PG 3:707f.
104. Galatians 2:20.
105. *De divinis nominibus,* ch. 4, par. 13, PG 3:711f.
106. Ibid., ch. 4, par. 19, PG 3:711ff.

Index

146

Fact, 34, 36, 38
Faith, ix, xi, xvii, xxv, 9, 13–22,
  26, 32, 35, 36, 61, 62, 84, 97,
  99, 101, 102, 104, 107–111,
  113, 114, 120, 127–129, 130,
  131
Farber, Marvin, xii–xvii
Feeling, emotion, 16, 27
Fides et Ratio (encyclical of
  John Paul II), xi
Figure (*Vorbild*), 96, 114

Gelber, Lucy, xvi, 136
God, 20, 21, 23, 29–32, 35, 39,
  40, 46, 49, 56–59, 62, 67, 69,
  80, 83, 85–89, 90–93, 95–119,
  122, 125–131, 142–145;
  arguments for existence of,
  21, 98, 126, 128, 145; as
  pure Being, 66, 77; as
  "theologian," 100, 104, 116,
  117, 142; human beings as
  image of, 35, 49; natural
  knowledge of, 57, 97, 98,
  100, 105–109, 111, 113, 118,
  125, 142
Good, 50, 53, 119, 120, 122,
  132–134
Grace, 21, 40, 107, 122, 126

Heidegger, Martin, vii, xi, xii
Hierarchy, order, 85, 86,
  115–116, 120, 132, 144
Holiness, 40, 90, 110, 129
Holy Spirit, 103, 114, 115, 119,
  141. *See also* God; Jesus Christ
Hume, David, 8
Husserl, Edmund, vii, ix, xi,
  xiii, xv, xix, xx, xxiv, 1–63,

81; *Ideas,* xiii, 33, 138;
  Logical Studies, 3, 37

Ideas, 76, 79, 80, 145
Image (*Bild*), images, 55, 76,
  90, 95–97, 99, 100, 108, 109,
  111–114, 116, 117, 121, 122,
  126, 130, 142, 143, 145; of
  God as fire, 90–91, 96, 97,
  11, 114, 125
Induction, 43, 44, 52
Inference, logical, 14, 44, 50,
  51
Ingarden, Roman, xi, 135
Insight (*Einsicht*), 17, 26, 41,
  43, 45–48, 50–53, 60, 63, 65,
  67, 106, 114; immediacy of,
  47–48, 50–53
Inspiration, 87, 102–105, 108
Intellect. *See* Understanding,
  intellect
International Phenomenological Society, xii, xiii
Intuition (*Anschauung, Intuition*),
  13, 14, 39, 40, 42, 44–47, 59,
  60, 65, 98, 106, 122, 123,
  126, 129
Isaiah, 103–104, 106

*Jahrbuch für Philosophie und
  phänomenologische Forschung,*
  vii, xi
Jesus Christ, 87, 90, 93, 95, 96,
  115, 117, 141, 144; incarna-
  tion of, 88, 117
John of the Cross, St., xxiii
John of Scythopolis, 85
John Paul II, Pope, xi, xvii
Judgment, 65, 72

The Institute of Carmelite Studies promotes research and publication in the field of Carmelite spirituality. Its members are Discalced Carmelites, part of a Roman Catholic community—friars, nuns, and laity—who are heirs to the teaching and way of life of Teresa of Jesus and John of the Cross, men and women dedicated to contemplation and to ministry in the church and the world. Information concerning their way of life is available through local diocesan Vocation Offices, or from the Vocation Director's Office, 1525 Carmel Road, Hubertus, WI, 53033.